And He said to me, "My grace is sufficient for you, for My strength is made perfect in weakness." Therefore most gladly I will rather boast in my infirmities, that the power of Christ may rest upon me. 2 Corinthians 12:9 (NKJV)

LIFE
IN THE
TURN LANE

LIFE
IN THE
TURN LANE

A Story of Personal and Corporate Turnarounds and
the Principles that Make Them Happen

Jim Patton

with Don Beehler

NEWVANTAGE
BOOKS

A division of New Vantage Partners
Franklin, Tennessee 37064
info@NewVantagePartners.net
Life in the Turn Lane
©2010 by James Patton
www.AmericasBusinessRepairman.com
Interior design by Wellspring Design and JV Design
ISBN 978-0-9816203-2-9
Printed in the United States of America
15 14 13 12 11 10   6 5 4 3 2 1

To Theresa and Spencer, who held on tight
during all the turns and supported me with
their unconditional love all along the way.

Contents

Foreword

W hen you look into the eyes of a business partner, a family member, a close colleague, or just someone you really depend on, there is always one trait you want to see: confidence. Not just confidence in you, but confidence in themselves.

As Jim Patton's son, I have had the unique privilege of looking into my dad's eyes on many occasions from each of those perspectives. And I can tell you one thing that is uniformly expressed from everyone that has known Jim: When life's inevitable bombs are falling in the trenches around you, Jim Patton is someone you want at your side.

Since this book largely focuses on the difficulties and triumphs of my dad's professional life, that is where I will focus the pages of this foreword. It should be well noted, however, that my dad's professional success did not come at the expense of his personal and family life. All too many businessmen reach the pinnacle of their career aspirations only to find themselves alone at the top, with no one alongside to celebrate their accomplishments. In my dad's case, while he went through many long days, stressful weeks, and trying years, he never lost sight of why he works in the first place—for his family. We will celebrate with him at the top.

The very first business influence I can remember my dad having on me turned out to be the spark leading to the career I am in now: investing as a hedge fund manager. When I was around eight years old, Dad wanted to instill in me his long-held belief in the importance of investing. As a guy that cut out physical bond coupons to cash at the bank before anyone even understood the concept of investing at least 15 percent of one's gross income, Dad had seen first hand the rewards one can reap through sound investing. With those beliefs in mind, Dad told me he would match, dollar for dollar, everything I put into the markets. Inspired by what an incredible deal this was, it was not long before all my birthday and Christmas money, allowances, and even spare change were being pumped into my brokerage account.

Dad taught me to look around, observe the business side of my surroundings, and take notice of more than just the surface world that most kids my age would see. It did not matter the companies that I bought. What mattered was the priceless education Dad encouraged me to pursue at such a young age. I learned what a publicly traded company is. In the process, I once even asked the waitress at our favorite, family-owned Mexican restaurant if they were publicly traded.

I learned what debt was, and I learned basic concepts like revenue, profit, and margins—priceless lessons that very few kids under ten years learn. And just so you'll know: I bought Disney (a major winner), Central Parking (major loser), Microsoft (winner), Cracker Barrel (flat), and Delta Airlines (loser) for my portfolio.

I love telling you my part of Dad's story, because as I now manage millions for investors in the stock, commodity, and currency markets, I never forget my roots. I can promise you I will be doing the same thing for my children, and I encourage you to find similar, inexpensive, yet fun ways to teach your children profitable lessons they will always remember.

Another great lesson that still affects me daily is one of simply showing respect to everyone. Whether it be to the cafeteria worker, the CEO, the janitor, or the wait staff, Dad always taught me to say "yes, ma'am" and "no, sir." To this day I love seeing the reaction from people who almost never get respect from someone they serve when I treat them as if they were my boss.

Dad taught me at a very young age that these people are no different than anyone else in the respect they deserve, the feelings they have, and, likely, the excellent work ethic they demonstrate each day. Dad said you can always tell a lot about someone by how he or she treats the wait staff at restaurants. Does that person show the staff respect? Does he or she take themselves too seriously and need to be reminded that nothing can be that bad when being waited on while others in the world starve? Thanks to Dad's lesson, I make it a point to take a potential business partner out to eat just to gain further insight into his character.

Perhaps one trait about my dad that has really shown through to me—and will unquestionably shine through to you in this book—is his creativity. Whether finding a way to get an eight year-old interested in stocks, a means of looking into someone's character, or a revolutionary way to close a deal, you can always see in Dad's eyes a creative spark about whatever issue is at hand. You'll benefit from this gift when you see how cleverly he shares the lessons of business life in the forty "Patton Principles" laced throughout this book.

Finally, I would be remiss if I did not mention the evolution of my father's relationship with God over the years. One of the prevailing themes I have observed in the business world is the profound absence of God in the lives of many of the most successful corporate leaders. Whether it is poor past experiences, ego, apathy, or any other cause, this is a widespread phenomenon. I believe the Jim Patton difference in this respect shines brightly. His faith and the way He walks with God is consistent not only in his personal life but in his public acts as well.

A spiritual leader of the household, as well as his community, my dad has taught me the real strength that comes from looking to God for guidance. I know, as he confesses frequently, that the success he has had in life would have been impossible without the profound blessings and love that our Lord has showered upon us. Dad has proved to be a good steward of what he was given, and I think the lesson of stewardship is a fitting way to conclude this foreword.

One of my favorite parables—not surprisingly, one related to investing—is Matthew 25:14-30. Take a moment to read and study these verses. I believe we all have opportunities in life to prove ourselves. Sometimes it starts small. Other times we get a big break—but we must seize the opportunity when it comes.

My father started with small opportunities and proved to be a good steward. Those successes paved the way for bigger opportunities, and my dad has literally reinvented the way distressed businesses are acquired and turned around. May you enjoy reading his life story as much as I've enjoyed being part of it!

Spencer Patton

Introduction

With a book titled *Life in the Turn Lane,* you might think I've spent my entire life going in circles. At times it certainly felt that way.

I made one turn after another, sometimes getting sidetracked by what appeared to be detours or dead ends, only to see, farther down the road, that these diversions were essential parts of my personal and professional journey. There were times I wasn't sure I'd ever arrive at my destination, and for many years I really didn't know where I was headed.

Maybe you've felt that way, too. Perhaps your life is going in circles or you've gotten caught in a detour. Maybe you are spinning your wheels or are stuck in a rut that doesn't appear to have a way out. It may be that you're just going through the motions of life because you've given up on ever attaining your dreams. If so, I hope you'll keep reading. My journey from a failed career as a heating and air conditioning repairman to being founder of a global private investment firm that restructures struggling manufacturing companies with billions of dollars in revenue had many turning points along the way.

One business publication referred to me as the "billion-dollar repairman," a title I would have found incomprehensible during the days I crawled under houses to fix faulty oil furnaces. I hated my job and wasn't particularly good at it. From a human perspective, my life appeared to be in a hopeless rut.

If your situation seems like that, ask yourself what sort of odds Las Vegas would give on an inept repairman carving out a successful career at acquiring, repairing, and selling failing subsidiaries owned by Fortune 1000 companies. And this a repairman who never spent a day in college and was completely unschooled in the principles of business.

In my mid-twenties, bursting with desire to succeed in my own business, I was willing to try just about anything. I dabbled in small businesses and worked hard but often made little, if any, profit. Perhaps you can relate, especially if you are having trouble making ends meet during these challenging economic times.

As you read my story, you'll find a series of critical moments of triumph and defeat that proved to be turning points. These times gave rise to the lessons and life axioms I learned and continue to live by today. In fact, turning around companies on the brink of being shut down is a metaphor for the many personal and professional turning points I've experienced.

I made many mistakes throughout my life and career, and in my haste to reach a particular destination, I sometimes ran past important stop signs I should have heeded. Enthusiasm and naïve optimism often clouded my judgment, resulting in painful consequences not only for me, but also for employees, friends, and family members. After years of saving for my first "big-time" deal, for example, I lost virtually everything, and my wife and I were forced to sell our home and move with our young son into an apartment. A defeat like that has a way of humbling a person for life, and it was a turning point I've never forgotten. As Walt Disney once said, "You may not realize it when it happens, but a kick in the teeth may be the best thing in the world for you."

Later, when I was back on my feet and buying manufacturing companies no one else wanted, I discovered that often the management of these failing organizations knew what needed to be done but were constrained by bureaucratic parent companies, which limited their ability to take appropriate action. In other cases, the existing management either lacked the experience necessary to make the right reductions in the size and scope of an operation, or it lacked the will to do so.

Empowering managers to make decisions and making difficult cuts where necessary were the "intensive care" needed to revive these companies. As a result of these and other common sense actions, when it came time to sell one of our companies, we often ended up with more employees than when we first took over.

Seeing this happen over and over again drove home a simple but profound lesson as to how much people can accomplish when bureaucratic hurdles—whether they come from the private sector or from government—are eliminated and employees are allowed to do the jobs for which they are trained. During a period when capitalism is under attack in many quarters, when millions of people are fearful and discouraged by an uncertain economy, and when our nation's manufacturing base is rapidly disappearing, this seems like a good time to share my story. I'm living proof that Americans have opportunities to overcome failure and achieve dreams that would not be possible anywhere else in the world.

The conversations recounted in *Life in the Turn Lane* are accurate to the best of my recollection. Some of them are as fresh in my mind as if they were spoken yesterday.

Interspersed throughout the book are my "Patton Principles" for business—and life—and chapters one through ten conclude with a "Turning Point" that embodies the lesson learned and the guiding principle or value. I also have a chapter called "Turning Wrong Turns into Right Turns", which examines a couple of big mistakes I made and how to avoid them.

The final chapter, "Learn from the Turns", summarizes the lessons and truths I learned through my career and provides practical application for readers. In the epilogue, I offer my thoughts on what it will take to revive America's manufacturing industry and make it competitive again on the world scene.

For readers interested in some of the more technical business aspects of my work, I've included appendices that explain more about how we do what we do. One details the factors involved in valuing a potential acquisition, and the other outlines my company's "One Hundred Days to Profitability" turnaround model.

By far, my biggest turning point was discovering that God loves me and has a plan for my life. The Lord did not always answer my prayers in the way I hoped, but He always did what was best for me. Some of you may conclude the positive turning points I experienced were coincidences or lucky breaks, but I know better. As I look back on my life so far, I perceive how many seemingly unrelated experiences were woven together in God's perfect design and timing.

For those interested in learning how to make a "you turn" of their own, the third appendix explains how someone can know God personally. Whatever professional success I've enjoyed pales in comparison to the joy of knowing Jesus Christ as my Savior and Lord, and to Him I give all the thanks, honor, and glory.

Jim Patton
September, 2010

A Turn for the Worst

"**S**on, you're just not any good at this."

Wrapping an arm around my shoulders as he spoke was the first real act of kindness my boss, George K. Jones, had shown me in the eight months I worked as a technician for his heating and air conditioning company in Athens, Georgia.

Almost from the beginning, I sensed he didn't like me. Perhaps it was because Mr. Jones quickly realized he had made a big mistake hiring me. I was lousy at fixing heating and air conditioning equipment, despite my two-year technical degree.

"My advice to you would be to find another industry to work in," he continued.

I stood there stunned, not knowing what to say, dreading what I was sure would come next.

"You are terminated as of this coming Friday. Please get your last check and take only your personal tools. Good luck to you, boy."

I stared away and nodded to let him know I understood what he had said. Mr. Jones turned and climbed the steps to his office. I listened to the stairs creak under his feet as I fought back tears.

Within my first year as a heating, ventilation, and air conditioning (HVAC) technician, I had just been pronounced incompetent at my chosen career and fired. Now, on a cold December day just before Christmas, I had lost my only source of income. Humiliation and panic hit me simultaneously.

While a part of me suspected this day was coming, another part hid in denial because I didn't know what else I could do to make a living. Crawling under houses in frigid or sweltering weather and battling spiders, snakes, dogs, and assorted vermin wasn't much fun, but it was what I had been trained to do. Truth is, I couldn't stand my job and, as Mr. Jones affirmed, I wasn't good at it, either.

Two years earlier, I was an HVAC equipment student at Athens Vo-Technical School (now affiliated with the University of Georgia). It was a strange place to be because I had never liked working with tools while growing up and being an HVAC student didn't change my natural inability to function with repairman's gear.

Oddly enough, my instructors never raised concerns about my lack of mechanical ability, despite my repeated demonstrations of poor aptitude for making repairs. A mechanic is supposed to think ahead like a chess player, but somehow that never quite worked for me. Whenever we had to take something apart and put it back together, I was always the student that had parts left over.

On one occasion, while working on an assignment that required soldering, I set fire to the insulation inside a wall. I thought I was going to burn down the school until another student and I managed to put out the blaze with a fire extinguisher.

If I had stepped back and taken an objective look at my HVAC abilities, I would have recognized the improbability that I would ever be happy or successful in the industry. But while growing up and then while at Vo-Tech, I never gave a great deal of thought to my future or what I wanted to accomplish in life.

Patton Principle

Deny denial, and face the facts. Refusing to own up to a problem—like being a terrible heating and air repairman while trying to do that very job—only makes it worse. The situation won't go away unless you take action. Better to get it over with than let a problem become a crisis that becomes a disaster!

I was born April 4, 1955 in Tucson, Arizona to an Air Force-enlisted father and a stay-at-home mother. In his twenty-year career in the Air Force, Dad started out as a military police officer and then worked his way into management as a non-commissioned officer in charge. He achieved this milestone in the record time of fourteen years and later was given responsibility for military inspections at bases throughout Europe. I remember he often brought us candy, nuts, or small gifts from his visits to other lands.

As the Cold War heated up in the 1950s and 60s, military bases were armed with nuclear weapons. They were expected to be ready for conflict, so Dad would fly from base to base for unannounced inspections to make sure everything was in order. Highly esteemed by his associates, my father, who passed away years ago, received numerous awards and recognitions for outstanding service, although he never said much about them. In fact, I didn't know of his many honors until my mother told me about them long after he retired.

Having a career military man as a father meant constant moving during my growing up years. Twice, my sister Helen and I spent three-year stints in Spain, but my oldest sister, Penny—nine years my senior—entered college in the states at the time of Dad's second European assignment. We also lived in many parts of the United States. With his family in tow, Dad was stationed as far west as California, as far east as Delaware, as far north as Montana, and as far south as Florida, where we relocated upon Dad's retirement from the Air Force.

My childhood consisted of a wonderful combination of life experiences in Europe and the United States, which taught me how unique people are and how beneficial it is to interact with different cultures. But no country in which my father was stationed compared to the United States. I have always been proud to be an American citizen.

One tremendous advantage of Dad's military career was that he got a full month of vacation each year. While in Spain, our family traveled extensively throughout Europe during those thirty-day breaks, so I got to experience the sights, sounds, and tastes of many European countries. I look back on those days with fondness and appreciate the benefit of growing up exposed to so many different people and places.

The downside to constantly moving was that up until my early twenties, I never had a friend—other than a cousin or two—for more than a couple of years. As a result, to this day I treasure every friendship, and some of my relationships go back twenty-five years or more.

Wherever we were living, my parents gave my sisters and me a weekly allowance in exchange for chores we were expected to complete. These responsibilities planted the seeds of a strong work ethic and also taught us the value of money. In time, we also worked outside the home.

One of my first jobs was to deliver movie schedules to housing areas on the military base. I would go from house to house dropping off the current issue, until one day I got the idea that I could make my life easier simply by burying the schedules, thinking no one would notice. Unfortunately, my father came along just as I was digging the hole to hide my first stash of them. To make matters worse, I lied to him about what I was doing. I couldn't sit down comfortably for the next couple of days and never again shirked a responsibility or lied to my father. This valuable lesson early in life foreshadowed how God would use the consequences of my decisions to mold my character for future business ventures.

Patton Principle 2 — Bury the temptation to be dishonest. Good character will cover a multitude of sins by helping you avoid them. Nothing you might gain in the short run through dishonesty is worth what it most certainly will cost you in the long run.

One summer, when I was about fifteen years old, I bought an electric lawn mower to earn some extra money cutting grass. I paid seventy-five dollars for it without considering how long it would take to recover my investment. As it turned out, I worked all summer to pay off the mower.

In addition, I soon discovered a cumbersome problem. Mowing a yard while avoiding the extension cord zigzagged through the grass added a frustrating amount of time to every yard I cut. On top of that, my inspector father would follow behind to check my work. He always found something I missed—an untrimmed corner or poorly edged sidewalk. Because he inspected military bases, I knew I wouldn't get anything past him during a lawn inspection, and I learned the importance of a doing a job right. Dad expected me to obey his every command, but I always knew he loved me dearly. My mom reinforced his work ethic by keeping a watchful eye on my house chores, making sure I really earned my weekly allowance of twenty-five cents.

My wonderful mother ("Mom" most of the time) likewise made her deep love for her children known in many ways. Her remarkable housekeeping featured cooking, cleaning, and providing a place where I always looked forward to coming so as to receive her warm hug and kiss. And she was a true 24/7 mom. When I was about ten years old, I often was afraid of the dark. For comfort, I would go to Mom and Dad's room, stand where (I thought) Dad couldn't see me, and motion for Mom to come lie down with me. She always did. My dad played his part well, too. He would pretend to be asleep, but knowing I was embarrassed to admit my fear to him, would mumble something about what I was doing. The giggles he set off helped me drift back to sleep.

After one especially bitter winter in Great Falls, Montana— less than an hour from the Canadian border—Dad decided to retire from the Air Force. I wasn't particularly sorry to leave Great Falls. To me, it had always felt isolated from the world and relentlessly cold. I still shiver as I remember wearing long johns in early spring during try-outs for the baseball team.

After leaving the Air Force, Dad considered several job offers but chose one in Ft. Lauderdale, Florida, with a former colonel to whom he had reported many years earlier. The colonel owned an auto collision center. His vision was to own ten or twelve of the franchises, and he wanted Dad to manage them and perhaps even become an equity holder.

Dad had never showed an entrepreneurial spirit, so I was excited for him about this opportunity. When we talked about the potential, though, he dismissed the possibility of taking equity in the company. He was only interested in providing for his family, as if the two were incompatible. While he had always been a good provider, it seemed to me that he limited himself by not having a larger vision for what could be rather than what was merely safe and practical. So, true to himself, he accepted the job but not the opportunity to become an owner.

The transition to civilian life in Ft. Lauderdale was a challenge for everyone in the family. I had just turned fifteen, and moving from Great Falls to Southern Florida, with its beaches and more liberal culture, was eye-opening. I felt I didn't measure up to my peers. I was skinny for my age yet taller than most. The height helped me letter in basketball and baseball in my freshman year, but it didn't help me with the girls. Other than sports, I didn't fit in. My school clothes were nerdy, I combed my hair wrong, and just about everything else, including my socks and tennis shoes, were outdated.

Like many boys my age, I delivered newspapers to earn extra spending money. I rode my bike to the local Publix store at about five o'clock every morning to pick up papers for my route. It happened to be the same time the doughnut delivery man arrived, and even then, my entrepreneurial orientation bubbled over. I worked out a barter arrangement: a box of doughnuts in exchange for a paper. The responsibility of having a newspaper route taught me the importance of being dependable, a lesson which has served me well throughout my career.

Patton Principle 3 — **Be your own best inspector.** People may not always see everything you do right, but someone will notice if you do it wrong. Once others know they can depend on you to do a job well, you're on your way to a life of success.

At fifteen, my learner's permit allowed me to drive until dark, so I got a job at a McDonald's near the beach, about twenty minutes from home. Part of a multi-store McDonald's franchise, the restaurant was owned by two brothers in Southern Florida. At the time, they were opening stores at a frantic pace and had difficulty getting new workers adequately trained to meet the demands of all their grand openings. To address the problem, the brothers created the "All-American Team." Team members were considered the best of the best of their employees, so no matter how many customers showed up at a store this team could meet their needs. Those who made the All-American Team received a quarter an hour higher pay and free hamburgers on opening day. Could it get much better than that, I wondered?

I worked hard and made the team, which taught me the satisfaction that comes from dedicating myself to achieving something and enjoying the recognition that comes with attaining a goal. The feeling so energized me that I inquired about getting into the company's management program. Much to my delight, I was accepted as the youngest member of the Southern Florida franchise management team.

Stepping up to management meant I needed additional training. Mom bought a tape recorder so I could record the year-long series of training classes. My recorder proved to be a great asset in studying for the many tests because at the time, McDonald's didn't have books or reference manuals for the training program. The recorder was one of many ways my mom stepped up and helped me chase a dream. Although always cautious, she would never stand in the way of me, my dreams, or goal-chasing in a sport or business.

As much as I enjoyed the track I was on at McDonald's, I was offered more money at a grocery store closer to home and ended up leaving the hamburger world to bag groceries. Unfortunately, I soon came to dread Saturdays and Sundays because baggers worked fourteen- to fifteen-hour days every weekend, and before we could go home, the floors had to be mopped and polished to a mirror finish in preparation for the next week of store traffic.

We'd lived in Ft. Lauderdale about a year and a half when my dad's uncle, who owned a successful real estate business in Athens, Georgia, asked my father to manage a new department within his company. The department was created to manage real estate properties for his customers, as well as other investors who wanted to retain ownership of their apartments or houses but didn't want the headache of dealing with renters.

Dad accepted the job and grew the new division from a few rental properties to more than eight hundred industrial, commercial, and residential properties. Even though my great uncle was very wealthy and got a lot wealthier thanks to my dad, he didn't have a sharing heart. He was overly frugal and paid miserly bonuses at year's end. This seemed to me an injustice given my father's hard work, and I determined at that point to be more generous if I ever had the chance. At an early age, I had learned how good it felt to give presents or money to family and friends, and as I matured, I experienced the blessings that come from giving to strangers.

Patton Principle 4

Give in to giving. Gaining by giving is counter-intuitive, but it works. The satisfaction of blessing others from your abundance is one of the greatest pleasures of "having it all."

Because my father's new job required him to move during the school year, my mother and I stayed in Ft. Lauderdale so I could finish my junior year of high school. Helen had just graduated, so she moved with Dad and found a job in Athens at the University of Georgia. Unaffected by our change, Penny had graduated from college years ago, married, and taken a teaching job in Minneapolis.

My big sisters could not have been better to their kid brother. For most of my early years, I was comforted to know that Helen was in the same school building. If I ever forgot something I needed during the day, I would just find Helen. Although she always reminded me sternly to bring my own next time, she would help me out and would defend me to anyone no matter the consequences to herself. Penny and Helen continue to be cherished examples of what it means to treat others as you would like them to treat you. They are still my models and mentors, and I love them both. They exemplify the best of what "family" can be.

By the time school was out I had turned sixteen, so my mother and I drove separate cars from Ft. Lauderdale to our new home in Hull, Georgia, just outside of Athens. Shortly after settling in, Mom took me to Danielsville High School to enroll me for my senior year. We found out that I could skip 12th grade and still graduate from Danielsville High School with a diploma if I agreed to continue my education by enrolling in a two-year technical school.

That sounded great to me. I had attended five high schools in less than three years and was not at all excited about going to yet another school where I didn't know anyone. In addition to sidestepping my senior year of high school, I was drawn to the potential of someday becoming self-employed. That's how I hoped to reach my life's goal of earning twenty dollars an hour. If I could make that amount of money, I thought, I would be set for life.

Excited at the chance to get a head start on my career, I enrolled at Athens Vocational-Technical School. It offered study programs ranging from medical technology to cosmetology, but I decided to pursue the HVAC program simply because I believed it would offer a secure job. Everybody's home needed to be heated, I reasoned, and once people get used to an air-conditioned house, they never want to give that up, either.

I was pleased to discover that Vo-Tech's HVAC program offered students the opportunity to work at their own speed, using written materials and videos. The instructors provided the equipment and established instructional challenges—removing wiring from a unit, for instance, so we would have to rewire it. To set up another "assignment," they might do something to cause a unit to malfunction, and we were left to figure out how to make it run again.

As was the case with most people in the working middle class, my parents' finances were tight, so I took a job after school as a janitor at Vo-Tech, working the second shift from 3:30-11:30 p.m. Within six months of starting work at Vo-Tech, I found a higher paying job, also on the second shift, at a place called Westclock, which was known for building the practically indestructible Big Ben alarm clock.

I muddled through trade school, knowing somewhere deep down that I didn't enjoy HVAC work, and the only time I "stood out" as a student was when I crashed and burned (sometimes literally) an assignment. Since I had never given college serious consideration and didn't think I had any choice but to continue my training, I pressed on and made the best of an unsatisfying situation.

Despite my limitations, I completed the program in eighteen months instead of the traditional two years, and although going to school and working forty hours a week was a heavy load for me, I was eager to graduate and get on with my life. I promised myself I would never work second shift again.

I was eighteen when the big day finally came, and I graduated from Vo-Tech. Ignoring the irony of my situation, I just knew success awaited me. I had a diploma from a high school I never attended and a two-year technical degree in HVAC—with a constraining asterisk that said "Oil Heat Only" because I had not completed the gas furnace component of the program.

Shortly after completing my studies, I landed an interview with George K. Jones, owner of an Athens HVAC company with a fifty-year heritage of serving the community. Mr. Jones's workforce of about forty employees was trusted throughout the Athens area for servicing used equipment and installing new units. Mr. Jones hired me based on the reputations of Vo-Tech mechanics that came before me. His previous Vo-Tech graduates were well qualified, so it was natural for him to assume I possessed the aptitude and skills for HVAC work.

The income from my new job enabled me to leave my parents' home, purchase a mobile home just down the road, and move into the same mobile home park where Helen lived. While I loved my folks, I felt the urge to establish my own identity. Now I had my own place, an old Chevy for transportation, and was closer than ever to my goal of making twenty dollars an hour.

I went to work for Mr. Jones on a spring morning, repairing home air conditioners and heaters. Eight months later, it was clear that that Mr. Jones and I had drastically underestimated my technical skills and aptitude, and there was no future for me in the HVAC repair world.

It never occurred to me then that God might have an alternate plan for my life. He was not much of a factor in my decisions during those years.

While my parents were moral, ethical people, they seldom attended church, and there was little "God talk" around our home. They taught me to be honest, to work hard, and to treat people as I would like to be treated, but said very little about having faith in Jesus Christ and seeking guidance from Him.

On the other hand, my father's mother maintained a powerful Christian faith and taught Sunday school for more than forty years. Yet for reasons I don't fully understand, her beliefs did not pass down through my father.

Mom made sure we attended church on Easter, and she evidenced some desire for us to know God by enrolling me in summer Bible School for a few weeks each year. Mom also kept a Bible available, but no one except Penny took much notice of it. As a young teenager, Penny became a strong Christian. For the most part, though, she didn't share her faith with Helen or me, because she had already moved out by the time we were old enough to think about it for ourselves.

Helen and I both accepted Jesus as our personal savior at the same time through a minister at the military base where my father was stationed. While I made a genuine commitment to Christ that day, I made no effort to grow in my faith. As I got older, preoccupation with school, sports, and work crowded God out of my life. As a result, I lacked a solid spiritual foundation, which worked fine for me—as long as things were going well.

Now, however, Mr. Jones had ripped the bottom out of my world.

Dejected, I trudged back to my mobile home after being terminated by Mr. Jones and flopped down on the couch. The events of the day had taken their toll; I broke down and cried like never before. Still, I gave no thought of turning to the Lord for help. Feelings of failure overwhelmed me. Christmas was just around the corner, and not only was I lacking money to buy gifts for my family, I didn't even have the funds to pay my bills past the end of the month.

I could think of only one thing to do.

Turning Point

Failure is often the foundation for success.

While my childhood jobs taught me some valuable lessons, I never took the time to evaluate my talents and natural motivations. I had a small vision and was content with simply having a job, regardless of my natural, God-given gifts and interests. Being terminated by Mr. Jones was humiliating and jarred my thinking about life and what I was best equipped to do—which sure didn't seem like very much. I was at a low point I had never experienced, and although I did not sense God's presence at the time, I see now how He used this situation to turn me around and steer me toward a life far beyond what I could have planned, hoped for, or even imagined.

Two Weeks that Turned My Life Around

"Hello, Dad."

"How ya doing?"

That was my father's special reply whenever he and I talked by phone. Not "how are you doing"—just "how ya doing?" I was glad he asked, because it gave me the opening I needed to break the bad news to him.

"Dad, I just got fired by George K. Jones."

"You didn't do anything wrong, did you?"

"The only thing I did wrong is I can't fix equipment as quickly as other technicians and sometimes can't even figure out how to begin troubleshooting. And I really hate it, anyway." Dad was sympathetic and said he had seen this coming, but he laid the responsibility for the predicament squarely on my shoulders.

"You and I both know you have to find another job quickly, because you're on your own now and are responsible for your bills," he said, as if I needed a reminder.

Dad also suggested that we get together to go over my budget and determine the bare minimum I needed to survive. We met at his home that evening for dinner and began calculating my expenses.

He had always been helpful in providing Helen and me a disciplined way of looking at economic realities. When I had moved out, Dad helped me come up with a list of expenses to anticipate and see how it stacked up against my income. Thanks to this exercise, I knew well what I needed to meet my obligations.

As a temporary way to pay my bills, Dad suggested I help him clean some of the apartments managed by his real estate rental company. Many tenants were college students or transient people, and they often left their units in a mess when they moved out.

Dad had recently inspected several apartments that were not in acceptable condition for new renters, so I could start work immediately. He told me which cleaning products to buy and put me to work at a rate of $150 to $200 per apartment. I discovered it typically took me the better part of a weekend to clean a single unit properly. Sometimes Dad would even change into his work clothes and help me clean an apartment. I think he enjoyed the time with me, and besides the companionship, I was grateful because with his help, the cleaning took half as long as usual.

Looking back, I appreciate Dad's practical help and regular encouragement, but I also appreciate the fact that he didn't try to fix everything for me. I learned to make the best of a difficult situation. I also quickly learned the pros and cons of being self-employed. While I enjoyed the independence, I had to provide my own insurance and tax withholding, and I experienced the challenge of not having a consistent level of work each week.

After I had been cleaning apartments for six months, Dad mentioned a possible opportunity he had run across with Rohr Industries. Rohr was a California-based airline manufacturer that had diversified into the mass transit business, building underground train systems. The company had just built a new manufacturing plant twenty-five miles away, in Winder, Georgia, where it planned to assemble three hundred trains for the new Washington, DC-area subway. Although I didn't realize it at the time, this was a risky stretch for Rohr to go from building airplanes to complex electrical trains.

Dad thought Rohr offered a good long-term opportunity and suggested I apply. He had recently rented an apartment to Rohr's human resources manager and said he would contact the man on my behalf—but only after I submitted an application and had an interview scheduled. Dad wanted me to experience the normal employment process without trying any shortcuts.

True to his word, Dad called the manager after I was contacted for an interview. His call paved the way for a second interview, where I was offered a full-time electrical apprentice job on the first shift for seven dollars an hour. Of course, I didn't mention in my interviews that I had nearly burned down Athens Vo-Tech during a wiring project, but as it turned out, my Vo-Tech background had nothing to do with the new job. I was elated because I had a new direction and was about a third of the way to reaching my goal of making twenty dollars an hour.

Patton Principle 5 **Put opportunities to work for you.** God often speaks through opportunities that just seem to come our way. If you pay attention and get on board, you'll discover the purpose and likely enjoy the personal growth it offers.

Shortly after I was hired at Rohr, two heavy-set, tobacco-chewing union representatives "encouraged" me to join the union, explaining that they would knock out my teeth if I didn't comply. Not wanting to get off to a bad start or incur unnecessary dental bills, I took their advice and signed onto the union.

At the time, my life revolved around work, so my knowledge of world and national affairs was fairly limited, as was my knowledge of finance and economics. I didn't follow any stocks or understand how the stock market worked, and I certainly didn't think on a state, national, or global scale. I simply went to work each day and looked forward to the weekend to go fishing, skiing, and camping. However, being part of the transportation union introduced me to a different world in the way of thinking and dealing with people.

The union's perspective had little to do with maintaining a healthy company that would sustain the hourly work force it represented. Rather, the union looked out for itself as if it somehow had a right to exist regardless of what happened to Rohr. But if unions were the way of things there, I determined to do what was required. Each day, I tucked lunch in my lunch pail and dressed in suitable work clothes—steel-toed shoes, safety glasses, hard hat, jeans, and a shirt.

Since my hiring had been done completely through human resources, I didn't meet my supervisor until my first day on the job. He knew I was coming, though, and had a toolbox waiting, filled with everything I would need for my assignment. My job was de-cabling overhead wires used in the train cars.

At the point where I was stationed, the cars were in the early stages of assembly. Each train started out as a separate vehicle, positioned on blocks. Overhead cranes moved the train from one construction step to the next. Cables hoisted each train and moved it down one assembly spot at a time. At the final point, the train was ready for a simulated "live" start-up just outside the mammoth doors at the end of the plant.

Back at my station—number two—each electrical cable began as a bundle so fat I could hardly put my hands around it. Inside the cable were forty individual wires, which I had to fit into a single giant electrical box. Once I wrestled a cable into the box, I had to stretch it so that each wire would reach its appointed destination. I then separated the individual wires, bending and cutting each with tools that allowed me to crimp and terminate any given wire at its final resting place.

Numbers in each cable corresponded to numbers in the electrical box, so I simply matched the numbers to make the right connections. My training was brief but to the point: "Find the matching numbers and pull that cable up far enough to be able to terminate your farthest wire."

Each car held at least fifty electrical boxes, and as soon as I finished wiring one box I moved on to the next. Usually by the time I finished wiring all the boxes, other work had also been completed, and the car was ready to move to the next station.

The Rohr plant housed fifteen stations in all. Assembly tasks began with the car's shell at the first station and concluded with a finished transit car at the last. To facilitate production, senior-level employees were always within walking distance, and I soon learned who to count on for help—and who not to.

Sometimes during lunch break, fellow employees invited me to join them at a table, but often not. I was considered a city boy and was not popular with my fellow employees, who mostly resided in the surrounding rural counties. Lunchtime conversations always focused on hunting, fishing, and college football games—and, not always delicately, women, of course.

I enjoyed working at Rohr because I could see and feel myself continually improve at my job. I also learned additional responsibilities as the days went by. It was a relief, after my awful experience with Mr. Jones, to find something I could do well.

My wiring skills were soon considered top notch throughout the division. After I finished, the wiring was always straight and tight, with no slack. As management noticed my work, I was moved farther down the line. That meant managers wanted my diligence in the more complex finishing areas of each assembly station.

For the first time ever, I felt I was good at a trade. I was proud of my role in the bigger picture of creating something that would run every day and carry commuters for decades to come. Nevertheless, I was keenly disappointed when, shortly after I was hired, I was moved to second shift because of the complex scheduling requirements for the train cars.

Patton Principle

6 **Appreciate the blessing of work you enjoy.** Sometimes work is drudgery, but when the times come (and they will) that you thoroughly like what you do, relish every moment. The more you find enjoyment in what you do, the more you'll find to enjoy.

About eighteen months into my job at Rohr, Terry, the first-shift supervisor, told me he was going on a two-week vacation and asked if I would take his place while he was gone. The assignment involved supervising fifteen union electricians. Still a bit short-sighted about what such an opportunity could mean, the main attraction for me was the chance to spend two weeks on first shift, so I readily agreed.

My status as a temporary supervisor required me to wear a white dress shirt and tie. I owned neither but gladly purchased two white shirts and three clip-on ties. When my former first-shift employees saw my sparkling white shirt and tie, they greeted me with disdainful laughter, which only increased the awkwardness I felt. The unwritten code allowed that a good union employee would never fill in for a supervisor, and they saw me as a bit of a traitor. They gave me a hard time every morning, but my troubles were just beginning.

About midway through my second day as supervisor, I was startled to see a small man marching rapidly toward me, glaring as he approached. Little did I know how much he would change my life.

Everyone in management feared 5-foot 4-inch, 135-pound Clyde Switzer, co-head of Rohr's Industrial Engineering Department in Winder. His department examined each job and the associated movements of the train to determine the optimum amount of time it should take a qualified employee to complete a task. There might be fifty to a hundred tasks measured in a time study. A task could be as brief as a few minutes or as long as an hour, but Clyde and his no-nonsense team never missed the slightest nuance of how best to perform a job.

As he swooped into my area, Clyde asked if I was the supervisor. Before I could answer, he announced he was starting time studies at my station and began barking orders.

"And everybody better conduct themselves just like they would if nobody were watching," he warned, sarcasm dripping from his words. "For two weeks, we're going to be in your face, looking at your work very closely with our study charts and stop clocks."

A study chart was a document that reflected management's best estimate of how much time it should take to perform functions necessary to complete work on the train.

Clyde spun on his heel and focused on me. It's a good thing Clyde wasn't a handshake sort of guy, or he'd have needed a towel to dry off after shaking my sweaty palm. He'd achieved his objective of intimidating me and was no doubt satisfied with how shaken I looked. I not only knew nothing about the time study scheduled for my area, but I had never even heard of one. Clyde was dumbfounded to learn I wasn't aware of the time study, much less prepared to assist him. I had stepped into a hornet's nest. By some coincidence, for two weeks—the precise time for which I was acting as supervisor—he and his colleagues would be scrutinizing my team's every move.

By day four of the study, my electricians' agitation over the industrial engineers' stopwatches and critical eyes was reaching critical mass. They realized that, for the first time, Rohr management would truly understand how much time it took the electricians to do their work.

It became apparent that the union or some of its employees, or a combination of the two, had padded the amount of time required to accomplish these tasks so the employees didn't have to work as hard. Once the true number of hours needed to get routine tasks done was determined by the time study, management would try to force employees to work within that timeframe. This, of course, would result in more conflict between supervisors and laborers.

By the end of the first week, tensions had peaked. I met with my team but didn't offer any sympathy: "I know what you have to do and how long it takes, and you know that I know, so get back to work." That went over really well, of course, and I silently wondered if it was okay to dial 911 for a dentist.

During the weekend, I reviewed the time studies and accompanying data. Only supervisors had access to such information, and I went over all the different functions with a critical eye, because I had done each of these tasks.

Knowledge is power, and with the knowledge I gained over the weekend and from months of working my job, I felt like Superman. On Monday morning, I was ready to face not only my fellow union workers but also the beady-eyed industrial engineers with their stopwatches.

Within thirty minutes, the first confrontation erupted between the union electricians and the engineers. Looking back, one of my proudest moments was to stare down these union employees. I told them in no uncertain terms that I knew all the tricks to drag out a task and that I expected them to do their jobs at the right rate without any padding.

"If you've ever done your job the right way, do it while they're checking us with stopwatches."

At that defining moment, I cut all ties and any friendships with my union co-workers without really understanding the implications of what I had done.

Shortly after my union confrontation, I met with Clyde. He assigned me the jobs he wanted to measure that week, along with estimated man hours.

"I'm going to show you, line by line, the time studies on each area. We're estimating 468 hours," Clyde said confidently.

Having already reviewed his estimates the previous weekend, I knew that some were a bit too long, others too short, and some way out of line. I told Clyde we could do the tasks in much fewer hours than he had in his projections.

"We can do this in 320 hours."

"We'll just see about that," he shot back, his wide, disconcerting smile showing off his shark teeth.

Patton Principle 7

Do your best every day — you never know when or where a big break will come. Pleasant surprises happen most to people who are diligent in their work. Although it often may not seem like it, the "right people" usually know what you're doing and will see that you get your reward.

Two weeks later, on a Monday afternoon, I was back on second shift, working out of my toolbox. The corridor became a gauntlet as I walked in to report for work. I was roundly jeered by those who were just leaving the first shift, and I wondered why in the world I had been foolish enough to put myself in that management position. It netted me only about two hundred dollars extra for the two-week period.

Terry thanked me for filling in during this critical period and revealed his secret. "I knew those time studies were coming, which is why I took my vacation then," and added a "gotcha" pat on my back. I didn't return his smile or friendly pat. I would rather have kicked him right where the sun doesn't shine.

I didn't have long to stew over Terry's deception before Clyde pounced once again. He stopped in front of me, looked me up and down, and yapped, "Patton, what exactly are you doing in those work clothes?" Even though I was a foot taller, his hot breath blasted me in the face.

"Mr. Switzer, these are my work clothes, sir."

"What do you mean, 'these are my work clothes'? You were the floor supervisor over station number two last week, were you not? What in the world happened? Did they fire you?"

"No, sir. I came from the second-shift electricians," I replied, explaining it was a temporary assignment.

Clyde couldn't believe it. "I've got something to show you. The work study results were 247 hours. Patton, you were right about it taking less time. You know all these jobs and how long they will take."

I don't know how I looked on the outside, but inside I was beaming. We had knocked off more than a hundred hours and greatly improved efficiencies during the time I was floor supervisor at station two. Saved time was the equivalent of "found money" for Rohr Industries. Still, I wasn't prepared for what followed.

"I want you to be an industrial engineering analyst and work for me," Clyde said, more from just thinking on his feet rather than having already turned in a requisition for a full-time employee in the industrial engineering department.

"I'd have to quit the union." I said.

"Of course you would, you idiot. I'd have to train you. Do you want it or not?" I could feel his hot breath bouncing off my forehead.

"Yes, sir, I want it," I said, hardly able to believe my ears. "How much does it pay?"

"Eight hundred dollars a week." Clyde said with a smile, knowing it was a lot more than what I was making as an electrician.

Eight hundred dollars a week, I thought, as I began making some mental calculations—why, that's twenty dollars an hour.

I had just reached my life-long financial goal. I remember at that moment wondering how long it would take to save up for retirement. I realized I had many years to go before rocking on the front porch with a wife and grandchildren running around, but I was getting closer.

Turning Point

My defining moment led to greater momentum.

When I took over as supervisor for two weeks, I had no idea it would pit me against my fellow union workers, or that it would lead to a promotion that put me on a management track the rest of my working life. When it came to the time study, I simply did what I thought was right, regardless of the consequences, and it became a defining moment for my career. Doing the right thing can simultaneously have both good and bad consequences, as it did in my case. But doing the right thing is never wrong. Even though my handling of the time study riled union co-workers, the ultimate outcome of the situation gave me the momentum I needed to go to the next level, strategically positioning me for my next significant turning point.

The Blue Collar Turns White

3

The Monday after Clyde hired me away from my second shift job, I stepped into the "doublewide" Industrial Engineering Department. The plant was not designed to house engineers and quality control people, so when Rohr won the contract to build trains for the Washington Metropolitan Area Transit Authority, management brought in doublewide trailers to house the engineering staff.

Clyde was at his desk when I walked in. He forced a smile, which quickly vanished as he resumed a phone conversation, snapping orders to the person on the other end. I stood silently, awaiting my orders.

Although not the designated manager, Clyde ran the Industrial Engineering Department. The department manager either attended meetings or holed up in his office most of the time. One of Clyde's first instructions to me was a warning: "Never trust those guys in production"—the department from which I had just transferred.

As the months went by, he proved himself a valuable mentor despite his considerably rough edges. Whenever we walked through the plant together, he pointed out potential areas for improvement. He once explained that storing raw material in an inconvenient spot required an extra fifty steps to transport it to the work area. By relocating the storage area, the department could save forty-five minutes per train car—an extraordinary savings of more than two hundred hours over the life of the Metro contract, with just one minor adjustment.

Another time, he showed me a work area without water fountains. He was convinced that the amount of time wasted by employees going back and forth to an adjacent section for a drink of water resulted in the loss of significant man-hours per month and justified the cost of installing an additional water fountain. A diehard time study expert, Clyde was always looking for ways to save manpower time, whether a few hours or just a handful of minutes.

Whenever Clyde gave me an analytic assignment, he insisted I report my findings in writing so he could share it with other managers. I quickly learned that, as an industrial engineer, I needed a good command of the English language to record my observations, such as the strengths and weaknesses I saw in production spaces, my suggestions for improvement, and the resulting efficiencies to be gained by implementing my recommendations.

Clyde quickly discovered the deficiencies in my writing skills. Each time I sent him a draft, he scribbled a barrage of corrections with his red marker.

"Patton, this paper you just produced is a piece of crap!" He hollered across the room rather than pull me aside for some private, corrective criticism. Others in the department heard every humiliating adjustment to my writing style:

"Too wordy!"

"Patton, don't use double negatives!"

I always knew by his growl when Clyde was working over one of my reports. Even when he wasn't shouting changes, it felt like everyone in the department could see the errors he exposed with his searing red marker.

By the time Clyde returned my drafts for revision, they looked like road maps. Nearly every available space was filled with comments such as, "Sentence is too long here"; "You changed subjects here"; "You need to reverse these two paragraphs"; or "SP" for a spelling error.

Although I cringed at his rebukes, I had no choice but to continue writing reports. I did my best to learn from Clyde's criticism and tried desperately not to repeat a mistake. My writing ability improved quickly, and I got fewer and fewer red marks.

Clyde was quick to criticize, but he was just as quick to recognize improvement. He often assured me that he could see my writing getting better and urged me to keep it up. He also relayed compliments whenever he heard good things about me from other people.

Despite his own, often overbearing, approach to people, Clyde taught me basic business etiquette and manners. One lesson I recall vividly was about the importance of showing respect. The way his office was positioned, he could see people coming in and out of the trailer from his desk. When the two of us would meet, he would have me pull my chair over to his desk, and if I broke eye contact during our conversation to see who was coming in, he would stop mid-sentence and say something like, "Hey, mister, look at me! It's rude to break eye contact when any Tom, Dick, or Harry walks into the trailer. It's very disrespectful."

That lesson stayed with me years later when I started acquiring companies. Maintaining eye contact not only shows respect for the other person, but also is an effective negotiation technique. Long after Clyde pounded the lesson into my head, I read a book about negotiating that encouraged holding out until the other party breaks eye contact. According to the author, that's the first round in any negotiation. It has proven to be a simple but effective approach I still use.

Patton Principle 8

Learn from everybody. Whether business etiquette, negotiating practices, writing techniques, or people skills, you can learn something from most everyone you work with. Each lesson prepares you for a better future.

In addition to what I was learning from Clyde, Rohr provided an in-house training program for employees interested in cross-training between departments. While the training was voluntary, Rohr offered an incentive by increasing the pay of those who were cross-trained. The training made employees more valuable because they could perform more than one job, and Rohr built a more knowledgeable and flexible work force.

Industrial engineering was one of the more complicated in-house programs. It included manuals and educational books similar to those found in a college library. The industrial engineering training required students to complete specific assignments and pass tests before proceeding to the next level.

Graduates of the program were awarded a blue name card to indicate that Rohr considered that person a trained industrial engineer. As my supervisor, Clyde had to sign off each time I completed a level. Although he was strict and stuck by the rules, I managed to earn my blue card after about a year and a half.

Within a couple weeks of joining the Industrial Engineering Department, I had been assigned to complete time studies. One of my first was to evaluate installing a junction box, the nerve center for various functions on a train car. The hydraulic junction box, for example, controlled all electronics that opened and closed the car's hydraulic valves. Another box included electrical switches dedicated to lane changes. Each car had about twenty junction boxes, and each one was critical to the individual train's proper operation and its functioning in unison with other trains throughout the transit system.

Because I had installed nearly every configuration of junction box, the electricians knew they couldn't get anything past me as I stood there with stopwatch in hand. Although I got dirty looks from union workers in many stations up and down the line, their disapproval was offset by the generally glowing feedback I received from management. I had started a new life, and I liked it very much. My once deflated self-esteem was slowly but surely recovering.

Looking back, I realize how my working conditions and circumstances with just a few fellow employees so easily affected my self-confidence. Because I was readily influenced, my self-assurance ebbed and flowed. It made me feel mentally weak, and it would be years before I would come to understand that I need to look to God as my one and only real source of stability.

Despite my successes, there continued to be opportunities to stay humble and be reminded of how much I still needed to learn. Industrial engineers were expected to draw accurate, basic mechanical and electrical applications. One day, I was asked to sketch a six-step wooden platform for production employees who needed a little extra height.

My drawing was off in a couple of dimensions, and the people in the Maintenance Department could have easily fixed my obvious error. Instead, they decided to have some fun at my expense and construct the platform to my exact specifications. The resulting first step was a whopping two feet deep and the next was three feet too high. A person would have needed a pogo stick to take those steps in stride, and I became the butt of jokes for several weeks. To this day, I pay very close attention to dimensions whenever I see a sketch.

Patton Principle

9 **Be confident, but know what you don't know.** Nobody knows everything—including you. That means you can "feel good about yourself" even when you're still learning. It also means you'd better use care every day to make sure you take account of your limitations. Otherwise, you and others who count on you may be sorry.

Every week, production managers, industrial engineers, and senior managers met to discuss the progress of each car on the assembly line. The meetings were held in a conference room with an oversized table and picture windows that overlooked the assembly space. My role was to update the production charts, which covered every available inch of space along the walls of the conference room. The charts showed the production scheduled for the week and gave an estimate of the percentage of completion for each car in each assembly area. At any given time, the plant had eighteen cars in process, which meant the plant was operating at capacity.

These engineering and management meetings typically were contentious, because usually there was disagreement about the degree of completion for each car as compared to what the conference room charts alleged. The presence of managers from the production floor as well as many different engineering classifications inflamed the weekly stress levels. These two groups routinely disagreed about how many hours it should take to complete a particular phase. This concerned the board of directors because the customer, Washington, DC Metro, was invoiced based on the wall charts, not on reports from the floor. In hindsight, it most assuredly should have been the other way around, but it was too late for that in mid-contract. Somehow, production had to catch up with what had already been billed as complete even though it actually was weeks and weeks away from being accurate.

The problem developed because production tasks got out of sync. For example, when a car moved from station six to station seven, in theory all tasks in station six were completed. In reality, however, the train was moved down the assembly line with some station six items still incomplete. This forced department supervisors to "chase" the train to the next station—sometimes even two stations down—to complete the work. Meanwhile, the clock started ticking on the next car to arrive in station six while workers pursued the unfinished train down the line.

There were people from almost every station chasing at least one car down line. No matter which station the car was currently located in, the production managers had to keep the cars progressing through the stations to stay "on schedule." This "derailment" was happening before the first passenger ever boarded or the first train ever reached Washington, DC.

Just as the further behind a student gets in a class, the more difficult it is to catch up, the situation on the floor worsened with each passing week. The managers knew assembling the cars was taking more time than planned, but they tried to hide how bad the situation had become.

The whole production line operated under great pressure to catch up, but overtime was frowned upon due to costs. That meant there was little a station supervisor could do but crack the whip harder to quicken the pace on the production floor.

The day of reckoning always came when a car reached station fifteen. There it was handled with white gloves, and quality control people swarmed each car to prepare for its first test run. When the reporting finally caught up with reality, though, the managers were thousands of man-hours behind.

Accurately estimating the cost to build something from the ground up—in this case, three hundred train cars—is difficult. Certain phases were in greater dispute than others when it came to allocating hours from start to finish. The electrical side of the cars was a significant part of the labor and expense, and accurately predicting time requirements was much more challenging due to the complexity of the tasks. Splicing and terminating thousands of wires, while installing major components such as seats, flooring, ceilings, and heating and air conditioning systems, was a mind-boggling task. Floor managers argued they were not allocated enough man-hours to complete the cars while management—motivated and measured by the profit and loss statement—dug in, insisting the hours allotted were adequate.

One week, the meeting started without me, because I was still not finished updating the production charts. Production management and the other engineering departments were well into a heated argument when I finally arrived. Clyde looked at me out of the corner of his eye and winked. He had previously let it be known that my production experience gave me a keen working knowledge of the time needed to complete specific electrical jobs. I didn't realize that his wink meant he was about to put me on center stage.

"Well, boys," Clyde said, interrupting the speaker, "it seems as if we have a resident expert in our presence. Jim Patton is industrial engineering's secret weapon.

"Patton, do you think car 186 is 58 percent complete, or less than 40 percent complete?" he asked with a smirk. Everyone hated Clyde's smile, because when they saw it, they knew he was about to devour them.

Since a mere 1 percent variance represented hundreds of hours of work, this 18 percent variance translated into thousands of man hours. If Rohr believed it had already paid for 58 percent completion of the production when, in fact, completion was at only 40 percent, heads would roll.

Everyone froze at Clyde's question. For the first time, someone in the room had information from both sides of the camp. I answered that car 186 was closer to being only 40 percent complete, and much to my surprise, no one challenged me.

Patton Principle 10

When you do know what you know, stick to your guns. Sometimes you know the answer everyone else needs. You serve others best if you don't back down, even if you have to stand alone for awhile.

During another management meeting someone shouted, "Hey, Patton, do you remember the time needed for this job from when you were still on the floor in production?"

"Sure," I said, "it only takes about thirty-seven hours to do that work."

The production folks went stone silent, because they claimed it should take an additional hundred hours.

I became such a good sounding board that even senior management valued my attendance in the weekly meetings to provide insight when a dispute arose. When asked my opinion I always told the truth, which often wasn't on anyone's charts because I found mistakes on both sides. It fascinated me that the managers always accepted my estimates.

No one ever challenged me in those meetings, largely because I had been positioned correctly when Clyde introduced me to the group. As a result, everyone accepted my input at face value. Through that experience, I realized that to be introduced as an expert and to have the knowledge to back it up provides instant credibility. Often the credence you're given will then carry over to other areas even if you start with a narrow field of expertise.

Even now, when my team works with an investment banker, we ask the banker to position our company, KPAC Solutions, to the seller as a credible purchaser of manufacturing companies, a buyer that carries through on its promises. I've learned that positioning our company strongly with a seller is vital, and that an introduction by a credible third party is the most effective way to get off on the right foot.

During my days at Rohr, I did not recognize that the education I was getting was one I would use for my own companies in years to come. Only God could have known that someday I would apply similar business formats and methodologies to improve efficiencies in manufacturing businesses around the world.

Patton Principle 11

Get a third-party endorsement whenever you can. To be introduced as an expert and have the knowledge to back it up provides instant credibility. It's always better to have someone else sell you than to try to sell yourself.

Assembly chugged along at Rohr until at last, finished train cars began to roll off the line. They were delivered to the Washington Metropolitan Area Transit Authority, two at a time, on a flatbed train. At that point, our work was further complicated by feedback from Washington that some cars were not operating properly in a number of areas. To make the situation even more stressful, by the time the cars arrived in DC, we had received hundreds of requests for engineering changes that had to be made on cars already delivered to the nation's capital. Those cars couldn't be returned to the Georgia plant, so Rohr was forced to develop a team to complete the change orders onsite in Washington.

Originally, before the first car was produced, both parties agreed to have engineering representatives onsite in Washington. That way, if Metro requested an engineering change, the representatives would work together to identify the cause of the problem, determine how many hours would be required to fix it, who would handle the work, and who would be financially responsible for the materials and man-hours to complete the changes.

For example, if Metro decided a car that needed to take a curve at thirty-eight miles per hour could only make it safely at thirty-three miles per hour, the fix for the problem had to be applied to all three hundred cars. That created a nightmare for the production people who already were crying for more time even without the modifications. However, it also created an opportunity to get enough additional hours so a few extra could be allocated elsewhere to relieve the strain on Rohr's production schedule. Otherwise, senior management tried to have any changes made within the original amount of time allotted for production, unless the customer agreed to pay for additional time to make the revisions.

As more and more cars arrived in Washington, the change orders piled up, adding to an already burdensome workload. The retro-fits were becoming more extensive and costly with almost every new car delivery.

"Who's going to pay for all these costs?" became a constant question. Rohr said it should be Metro because the engineering change orders were not part of the original contract. Metro had agreed to the specifications used for the cars, and the problems that took place in Washington didn't occur during Rohr's testing. Metro, of course, had an entirely different point of view, saying that the engineering changes were required, because the Rohr trains failed to perform as originally designed for Washington's climate and topography.

As the head-butting between Rohr and Metro became more frequent and intense, it came as no surprise when Rohr was not awarded another contract to build more transit cars. A serious disappointment for Rohr, the company had hoped to convince other major cities to purchase and install above- and below-ground rail systems like Washington's.

With the lack of any additional production contracts, Rohr's management knew that when car number three hundred rolled off the production tracks, the labor force was done. Now, as worried workers looked for other job opportunities, Rohr faced a mass exit of knowledgeable employees before the last car was manufactured, quality checked, and shipped to Washington.

Because each employee was badly needed to complete the three hundred cars on time, Rohr offered generous severance packages to key employees who committed to stay. If Rohr missed the completion deadline, it faced stiff penalties for each day it ran over.

Once again, my extensive production knowledge worked to my advantage. I was offered one of the last positions in the Industrial Engineering Department, and as a result, more and more authority rested in my lap as senior employees either returned to Rohr's headquarters in California or found other jobs nearby.

One day, I was called into a strategic meeting as car number 295 moved down the production line. The end was coming soon, and the meeting focused on Metro's abundant, frustrating, engineering changes, which by this time had come to the attention of Rohr's board of directors.

The estimated cost of completing the engineering changes in Washington was staggering, and the management group asked me if the strategy used to calculate the hours required to make the repairs was fair to both sides. Unfortunately, my findings (not official by the stretch of anyone's imagination) were not favorable for Rohr. I concluded Rohr was to blame for many of the necessary changes. My assessment didn't surprise the more realistic managers because some of the required changes had actually been instigated by Rohr prior to Metro even seeing the cars or testing their performance on the tracks.

As the end was coming down the track inside our plant in Winder, Georgia, management asked me to spend the next four to six months alternating between DC and Georgia in two-week intervals. At this late stage, I was the only industrial engineer at either location. Even Clyde had been let go.

Clyde and I had said an emotional good-bye. He had come to care for me like one of his sons (he had two), and I think he was proud of my achievements, although he rarely showed the love he felt for me. I, too, loved Clyde and thanked him constantly for my job. Eventually Clyde tried to stop my overly verbal gratitude, "Enough already! You're welcome, you're welcome!" But I kept on thanking him anyway during that last eighteen months or so.

During my back-and-forth months, I tussled with Metro representatives. Although my first two weeks in Washington went smoothly, things became gradually more adversarial. Eventually, we came to agreement on 500 of the 530 outstanding change orders. Rohr management was delighted with me, and Metro was happy enough not to sue Rohr on those particular items—at least for the time being. After I left Rohr, I learned that the lawsuits started flying from both sides.

Once again, I found myself looking for a job, but I had come a long way from my days with the union. With all I had learned, my confidence soared. My knowledge of manufacturing and my role as a trusted sounding board for management made me a more positive, forthright, self-confident person. Nevertheless, I was careful not to forget my beginnings.

I didn't know what was in store for me next, but I knew I needed to find out—and soon.

Turning Point

Two things helped me move into a critical role in Rohr's Industrial Engineering Department:

Having a willing mentor and being a willing learner. Everyone needs a Clyde early in his or her career, and I was fortunate that Clyde saw potential in me and was willing to teach me everything from corporate etiquette to crew efficiency. From manners to management, Clyde made sure I understood the in's and out's of our business, and it benefited both of us. But as big a turning point as Clyde's help was in my career, equally important was my willingness to learn from him. It would have been easy to be put off or offended by his rough manner, but I realized quickly that Clyde meant well and that I would do well to listen to him. As a result of his encouragement and the progress I made in that year and a half, the confidence I lost after being humiliated by George K. Jones was restored by Clyde Switzer. Today, I always try to build people up and increase their confidence by encouraging them and treating them with respect, because I know from first-hand experience the effect of someone's investment of the same in me. As will become apparent throughout this book, God was preparing me in ways I could not begin to imagine. He never wastes an experience in life, and many of the things I learned at Rohr have been invaluable to me throughout my career. While we can't always make sense of what happens in our lives, if we put our faith and trust in Jesus Christ we can be assured that He will guide and direct us for our ultimate good.

4 Turning against the Tide

When word got out that Rohr's contract with the DC Metro was not renewed and that some of its top talent at the Georgia plant was soon going to be out of work or moving back to California, headhunters showed up like sharks in a feeding frenzy. Because Rohr had planned that I would be the last person in the Industrial Engineering Department, I was rewarded with extra severance pay to stay until the final train car was completed. Although the trade-off was that I had less time to look for a new job, my wallet had extra money in it to make the period of unemployment less stressful.

A few weeks before my job ended at Rohr, I interviewed with a headhunter named Tony. One of his clients was Keene Corporation, a manufacturer of filtration devices, especially known for its airline fuel-filtering device. With manufacturing plants in LaGrange, Georgia, and Greeneville, Tennessee, Keene was looking for a product engineer to help its Engineering Department in LaGrange. The company hired me to find replacement materials for one of its filters in order to make the filter easier and more cost-effective to manufacture.

I wish now the job description had been better defined. There was no written document, just some general verbal input.

Shortly after starting my job at Keene, I put together a list of potential filtration materials as I thought I was supposed to do. But when I showed my list to the plant manager, he told me, "I'm not really sure why they hired you, because I have been making this product for about thirty years. We've tried every known product alternative for this filter."

Although I had thought this job was similar to my previous work, I began to realize that the appropriate background for what the company really wanted to accomplish would have been someone with an education in chemistry and a background in laboratory testing and analysis of raw material components. I did not have that education or experience, nor were the real needs discussed in my job interviews.

In the months that followed, it became increasingly clear my position was unnecessary. Management figured that out, too, and within six months, I was offered a promotion to move to the Greeneville plant, a larger operation that manufactured many different products. I turned down the job, though, because I didn't want to move farther north or to live in a miniscule town in the Smoky Mountains. So Keene terminated me on Christmas Eve, just ten months after I was hired.

It was Christmas season again and no job. But this time, I wouldn't have the "dry spell" that followed my HVAC termination by Mr. Jones. I contacted Tony again, and he was glad to have the chance to sell me to some other company. Before long, I had a job as an associate engineer at Roper Pump Corporation in Commerce, Georgia.

12

Don't let déjà vu scare you. Even if a "bad experience" seems to repeat itself, remember that you've probably learned a lot since the last time you faced a situation like it. Chances are, your resources and networks have grown, so consider it an exciting time to see what your next step forward will be.

At the time I started work at Roper, the company produced a wide range of pumps, among which was a market-leading product line, unique in its applications. The division I worked for produced these "progressing cavity" pumps, commonly called "screw pumps."

The pump's stator (the stationary part of the pump housing) and rotor resembled a classic red-and-white barber pole, and its exceptional design made it possible for a variety of industries to use it for transporting a wide array of materials. Screw pumps could move anything from fragile, whole fruit like cherries (which would be damaged if processed through a traditional pump) to the decidedly un-fragile sludge from sewage treatment plants.

My responsibilities included collaborating with mechanical engineers to write complicated operating manuals and specifications for using certain heavy-duty pumps. As difficult as they had been to endure at the time, Clyde's verbal thrashings over my writing style and grammar had greatly improved my written communication skills, which now were critical to my writing of these technical documents.

13

Be thankful for hard lessons learned. Through the eyes of faith, "God never wastes anything." When you see how a hard time prepared you for current success, be grateful to the One who brought you through it—and be glad there's at least one tough lesson you hopefully won't have to repeat.

One of the more interesting aspects of my ongoing training at Roper was to work in the plant a couple of days each quarter, a mandate by upper management for all salaried employees. Unlike many others, I looked forward to those days because I got out from behind my desk and into the manufacturing area. I would don blue jeans, safety shoes, and glasses and spend the day in different parts of the plant on a pre-arranged rotation.

I soon became friends with the supervisors and hourly workers; my heart had felt a connection with manufacturing processes long before I joined Roper. My interpersonal skills had been honed at Rohr, and it was easy for me to work alongside the employees who built the progressive cavity pumps supported by my department.

During my time in the plant building pumps, I became equally comfortable with specifications for each of the hundreds of pumps manufactured by Roper. The product line was in such demand that customers waited up to a year for delivery. This time delay was manageable for customers through long-term planning of the construction process. Roper replaced worn or broken parts in the field to make the exceptionally long lead times more palatable.

I spent hours each day talking with customers by phone and helping installation contractors. Through these conversations, I discovered what I needed to know in order to obtain the exact materials necessary to assemble the pumps, to specify adequate horsepower for pumping material up, down or sideways, to determine the distances through which the product had to be pumped, and also to communicate how to properly install the pumps. I often talked with people who knew nothing about pumps or how to determine the size needed for a given task, yet the materials they wanted to transport required exacting standards.

The variety of pumping situations kept my job interesting every day. In some cases, customers needed to pump thick, mucky stuff two stories high. Others required short-range, delicate movements. There seemed no end to the varying applications and challenges I had to calculate. Sometimes I consulted with other Roper engineers, sometimes the architect involved, and usually a supporting cast of experts in specific fields.

Understanding what material was to be pumped was just the first step. I then determined whether temperatures and possible changes in the material as a result of the pumping action had any bearing on the pump specifications. The viscosity of what needed to be pumped could be as thin as water or as thick as cold molasses. Once I had all information in hand, I could zero in on the pump specifications best suited for a particular application.

In addition to engineering challenges, as with Rohr Industries, I found myself in the middle of labor disputes. One particularly nasty episode erupted over wages and benefits, and the union called for a strike. I joined about twenty office managers—including people from engineering, scheduling, and quality control—in crossing the picket line so we could take the place of striking workers in building pumps.

Each salaried employee had to decide for himself whether or not to cross the picket line. Some chose not to out of fear of retribution, and understandably so. The hourly employees were indeed unhappy to see us cross the line, which they had formed across the plant's only parking lot.

Progress was slow, but we picked up speed with each new pump as we learned by doing. One of the challenges in assembling these heavy-duty pumps was that each assembly bolt had to be torqued to a specified level with a torque wrench. The wrench itself had to be calibrated regularly to insure accuracy, and there was a bit of an art to using it.

When pressure was applied to the wrench, a meter on top indicated when the bolt had been tightened to the proper level. Once tightened to specification, each bolt was covered with a wax seal similar to the king's seal of old. If the bolts didn't have wax on them, the user knew that pump hadn't been torqued. In addition, different colored waxes were used at various stages of assembly, and the Quality Control Department added its own bright yellow seal of final approval.

We discovered that, right before they went on strike, the union workers had waxed pumps which hadn't yet been torqued, so as to disrupt us. We had to peel the wax off all the bolts and start over as there was no way to know which had been torqued and which had not—a labor-intensive task since there were about forty bolts per pump and forty pumps that had to be re-torqued (1600 bolts in all!). In addition to the torque problem, we also found a number of partially assembled pumps that union workers had intentionally equipped with the wrong rotors and stators. Had we not uncovered this sabotage, it would have created a major snafu for Roper and damaged our reputation. It also would have bogged down customers who were counting on those pumps to meet their own production schedules.

Thanks to Roper's ongoing training practices, we had worked in different parts of the plant and had some experience with each phase of production. Even so, a seemingly simple task such as sealing wax on bolts can be a challenge for someone who doesn't do it every day, to say nothing of the difficulty for a bunch of inexperienced managers running a floor-mounted router or a large drill press. Despite these struggles, we did our best to keep up with the production schedule, because customers were counting on getting their pumps, and some had already been waiting a year.

One day during the strike, a U.S. military order surfaced that included among the paperwork a folder marked "top secret." We stared at one another, wondering what to do with the folder. Were we supposed to open and read it as part of the process or just ship it unopened with the pump? No one wanted to run afoul of clandestine military operations, so we decided not to open the top-secret folder.

For this mysterious pump, we were handling steel supplied by the military. We mounted the material on a lathe and started trimming it to get a properly curved rotor, which in turn created a progressive cavity through which material eventually would be pumped. Steel shavings showered the floor as we lathed.

A normal part of the process, the shavings at first collected on the ground without notice. Soon, though, our eyes widened as smoke began drifting up from the coating of steel fragments on the ground. The heat intensified, so we sprayed the burning material with a fire extinguisher. We were dumbfounded when the extinguisher did nothing to cool them off, and the shavings started burning through our floor.

The machinist turned off the lathe, and we stood there scratching our heads, trying to figure out how to cool down this mystifying substance. We watched as the glowing shavings burned through the wood and began working their way through the cement. That really had us worried because important plumbing lay beneath the concrete subflooring.

Near panic, we decided to risk opening the top-secret folder and found a document explaining that the material was an off-the-record steel alloy. The document didn't tell us what material would be transmitted through the pump. Only that it was so corrosive this special steel was required to contain it. When shaved on a lathe, the secretive file explained, metal fragments heat up and could only be extinguished with a special powder the military had sent along in an unmarked box.

After a mad scramble, we found the box, scooped out the powder, and followed detailed instructions on how exactly it should be sprinkled over the metal shavings. Once we had covered the shavings with powder, we were to dowse it with a liquid, which to our surprise caused the material to encapsulate itself. Finally, the instructions warned us to ship everything back to the military—including the cocooned scraps—along with any leftover powder. We also were forbidden to do a chemical analysis on any materials associated with this top-secret project.

Patton Principle **14** **Before all else fails, read the instructions.** Some problems stay small if you pay attention to what others already know about solving them. The old saying is true: "Anyone can learn from his own mistakes. The wise man learns from the mistakes of others." If there's a known way to do something and avoid pitfalls, do it that way!

By the time the strike ended four weeks later, the managers and engineers recognized the significance of that month of hands-on experience. We had gained a valuable new perspective on the manufacturing process and how much time it really took to build a pump.

The strike provided me one of many opportunities at Roper to develop deeper insights into how a business operates in the areas of manufacturing, distribution, and finance. With my earlier experience at Rohr and my interaction with Roper's customers, I began to understand operational patterns in a manufacturing company selling to a distribution network. My interaction with so many small- and medium-size businesses— both distributors and their dealer networks— also revealed that many owners did not understand their own financial statements.

This lack of understanding extended to the interlocking relationships between the profit and loss statement, balance sheet, and cash flow statement. At the time, though, I didn't recognize my own need to learn about financials, because they had little to do with my specific area of responsibility.

After nine months at Roper, I also recognized something else happening in me: I was getting bored. I yearned for something more than just a technical support job within the Engineering Department. I thoroughly enjoyed manufacturing and didn't want to do anything else I could think of, but to advance further on my current path I would need an engineering degree. Yet I had no desire to pursue that or any other direction that would require going back to school and earning a degree. Although I was just in my early twenties, I felt too old to go back to school, and other business opportunities I explored either were too expensive, required additional training, or meant I would have to break into a new industry. I felt stuck in a rut, and while I didn't know what direction to take with my career, there was no doubt in my mind that returning to the same old desk with the same old chair in the same old manufacturing plant was a dead end.

Then, while visiting my family one Thanksgiving holiday, my mother overheard me tell one of my sisters that I was thinking about embarking on yet another job search. Her eavesdropping was timely. Mom had a friend whose son was in management with Rheem Manufacturing Company, a national manufacturer and distributor of heating and air conditioning equipment, and she thought working there might offer some potential for me.

Rheem operated plants in Arkansas and Alabama, with distribution across the entire United States. Her friend's son was Tom Howell, who lived and worked out of a regional office in Richmond, Virginia. An up-and-coming marketing manager, Tom worked with independent distributors in the eastern United States.

I immediately perked up and told Mom I would like to speak with Tom. She thought he was in town for Thanksgiving and gave me several phone numbers. With no regard for his privacy, I decided to call Tom over the holiday to introduce myself and explore the possibility of getting a job at Rheem. I caught him on his way to visit his mother and quickly discovered he was not in the least impressed with my inappropriate timing.

After giving him a rapid-fire introduction in which I explained how I got his name and my qualifications for working at Rheem, he asked, "Do you realize this is the Thanksgiving holiday?"

"Yes, I know that, but I really don't like my job," I replied.

Calling Tom at Thanksgiving was a bad idea, but despite this rocky start, he agreed to get together if for no other reason than to meet the guy who had the gall to phone him on a business matter during a holiday. We met a few days later, just prior to Tom's return to Richmond. As we reviewed my resume and experience, he saw that I had a good grasp of how to sell through distributors and the dealership network under the distributor.

Patton Principle 15

Know when to break the rules—and how. Sometimes calling at an unusual time (during a holiday, for instance) communicates legitimate urgency and concern. But sometimes, it's just bad timing—and rude. If you're going to break a rule or social custom, make sure it's going to be received the way you intend. Otherwise, don't do it.

Rheem sold its products through a national network of independent distributors, and Tom realized I understood the mentality of distributors and the complexities of making this arrangement work smoothly. Tom also anticipated that my HVAC certification would bring me credibility with the dealership network.

About a week later, he contacted me to say he would recommend me to his boss, Randy Nichols, as a potential manufacturing representative for the company's Ruud brand. Ruud was identical to the Rheem line except the units were painted a different color. (Rheem was neither the first nor the last HVAC company to follow this marketing ploy. It worked so well that Carrier—by market share the largest commercial air conditioning manufacturer—offered four "different" product lines. All four brands were manufactured at the same plant but painted differently and given different brand names. The strategy behind this approach was to lead consumers to think they had a meaningful choice among HVAC units.)

Tom explained that my territory would be centered in Nashville, Tennessee, but before he talked with his boss, Tom wanted to know if I would be receptive to moving there. I asked him about the pay, which turned out to be several thousand dollars more than I was currently making, and when he added that I would also get a company car, a generous commission plan, a benefits package, and expense account—along with the added perk that I would work out of an office at my home— I eagerly agreed to take the job if it were offered to me.

The plan Tom outlined stirred my imagination. Since my days in the filtration business with Keene, I had been exposed to the salesmen who called on my employers. At times, a sales rep would take us to lunch, which was a tremendous treat to me at that stage of my life and career. In several years, I had been invited perhaps four or five times to eat out on someone's expense account. Now, it looked as if I was about to be the one with an expense account, something I had actually dreamed about having someday.

Following Tom's recommendation, I had what seemed to be an extremely positive meeting with Randy, although, as with my introduction to Tom, it didn't start off in an ideal fashion (so to speak). I had bought a suit for the occasion, and the fabric had a conspicuous sheen to it. I really thought I'd done a great job of dressing to impress, but Randy thought differently. He took one look at me and commented that he hoped my other suits (I had no others!) were more conservative than the shimmering specimen I was wearing. He strongly hinted that my customers wouldn't like it, either.

Once past the shock of my attire, Randy seemed impressed with my background and knowledge of the heating and air conditioning business. In particular, I struck a chord with my understanding of the manufacturers' constant struggles to gain market share, the vital role of unit-pricing, and the distinctives of Rheem's distribution strategy. Like Tom, he also recognized that I understood HVAC equipment even though I was quick to point out I wasn't any good at repairing it.

"None of us can repair the stuff," he responded. "We just need to be good at getting people to sell it for us. There are plenty of others competent to repair them."

Within days, Tom called and confirmed that my meeting with Randy had gone well. He had given Tom the thumbs up to hire me. Everything was looking good, Tom told me, and he ended the conversation by saying he would be in touch.

Then, silence. Weeks went by, which seemed like an eternity. How long could a little paperwork take, I wondered? I decided to call Tom, and he assured me everything was fine and that a job was in the works.

Then, more of the same. Several more weeks passed, and by now it had been two months since my meeting with Randy. I convinced myself the job was never going to materialize and grew angry at Tom for having gotten my hopes so high for nothing. I felt insulted and dismissed the hopes and dreams I had for this new job. It was an immature reaction, but I didn't realize that at the time.

Finally one day while working in the plant I heard, "Jim Patton, line one," over the intercom.

"Is this Jim Patton?" the caller asked with an enthusiastic tone as I picked up the phone.

"Yes, sir," I said, thinking it was a customer calling about another pumping application.

"This is Tom Howell, Ruud air conditioning."

Before he could say another word, I slammed the phone down and walked away. I had written Tom off and was convinced this was nothing more than a courtesy call to tell me I hadn't gotten the job.

"Jim Patton, line one," I heard a few seconds later.

"Hello, Jim, this is Tom! Did you just hang up on me?" Tom said with a pointed emphasis on the word "me."

"Yes, I did," I said as I again slammed the phone down.

As I started walking away I heard, "Jim Patton, line one. Gentleman is upset."

The receptionist's words were a warning to me that management was starting to notice I was acting rudely to someone, and it better not be a customer on the other end.

At that point, it dawned on me that I might have made a terrible mistake. Maybe he actually was calling to hire me.

"No one hangs up on me like that, young man," Tom thundered as I took his call for the third time. "You have an attitude, son, and you had better lose it quick, or I will be the one who does the hanging up. I assure you, if you hang up again, you and I are finished. You understand me, Jim?"

"Well, Tom, I thought you were going to say the job had gone to someone else," I responded sheepishly. "I was heartbroken and didn't want to hear it. It is a dream job and I just hated to have lost it."

"Well, you shouldn't treat your new boss like that."

"You mean you were calling to offer me the job?"

"Yes. I'd like you to give your notice today, if you trust me, because a letter of confirmation is being sent today to your home address."

He went on to say that assuming I accepted the job I should plan to report to work December 1. The year was 1979, and my career was about to take another major turn. I accepted his offer and was hired as Rheem's youngest-ever marketing representative.

Patton Principle 16

Never, never, never, never, never be rude—never! Everyone has reasons for doing what they do. Your job is to treat others as respectfully as you can. Even if you think you know they're being unkind to you and your rudeness is justified, you also might be wrong about that, and sorry later.

My work with the Ruud distributors went smoothly, and within a few months, Tom sent a letter to me saying, "Jim, you have eclipsed by far the main hurdle, which is having the distributor base find you acceptable and credible. Among shining stars, you are indeed a bright one."

In less than five years, I had come from being a demoralized, terminated heating and air conditioning repairman to a successful Ruud representative in several southeastern states. Happily, Rheem's incentive plan doubled my base salary if the distribution network in my assigned territory increased revenues to a specified level. As promised, I also was issued a nearly new company car that I would trade every few years according to company policy. All gas, maintenance, and insurance were provided by Rheem.

I grew to love the flexibility of working from my office at home. I set my own schedule for sales calls, driving or flying to visit the distributor network every six weeks or so. I felt I truly was "moving on up" in the world, which pleased me to no end. (I didn't realize how inexperienced and naïve I would have seemed in big business places such as Chicago and New York City, but I wasn't there—yet.)

One of my most important tasks at Ruud was to maintain the confidence of the established distribution network. On a particularly memorable occasion, my boss and I had to inform a long-time Rheem distributor in Charlotte, North Carolina, that he was being switched to the Ruud line. This didn't happen often, but when it did, sparks usually flew.

The Rheem distributor—whom I'll call John—was in his fifties and had been in Charlotte for many years. To say he was a stereotypical country boy was an understatement. Ken Geurian, my boss at the time, and I took him to an upscale restaurant to break the news to him, which in hindsight probably was a mistake. Our meal included escargot, and at one point John hollered to the server, "Hey, bring me some more of those snail pot pies."

Despite his obvious enjoyment of the meal, John was not at all interested in switching to the Ruud brand and tried to impress us with his vast experience as a Rheem distributor. Nevertheless, the decision was out of his hands.

To persuade him to make the switch without too many ill feelings, we agreed to provide advertising money so he could notify the marketplace about this significant change. We also provided funds for converting signs on the trucks of his well-established contractors who installed the products. We even agreed to pay for dinner meetings with dealers and contractors to explain the switch. Although John and his contractors resisted our plan, the change ended up working out well for all concerned.

The experience increased my appreciation of the cost of rebranding in both man hours and the actual outlay of funds. And seeing firsthand the challenge of persuading people to switch from an established brand to one that is perceived to be a step down (even though the only difference is the color of the product) gave me a greater appreciation for the power of marketing.

In addition to career advancement at Ruud, my personal life took a wonderfully positive turn. While having dinner with a tennis friend and his wife one evening, the conversation turned to my bachelorhood, and before I knew it, I had my first blind date. Theresa Ann Gannaway was the sister of my tennis friend's wife, and it was Theresa's first blind date, too. And for both of us, it was our last. Three years later, in May 1983, Theresa and I were married.

Within a year or so, the flexible schedule I enjoyed with Rheem fed my entrepreneurial appetite. I became so productive I was able to do my job in fewer hours, and unknown to Rheem, I often had many hours of down time. Rheem knew the logistics of the territory for my contemporaries and me, and the shape and overall size it covered naturally created idle time. Rheem, though, had no idea just how much down time the reps had over a month's period because there were many ways to account for a day's work. I knew I could have been more productive by making introductory calls and doing competitive analysis, but my work ethic was warped by my entrepreneurial leanings rather than working hard for my employer.

I am ashamed of it now, but I took advantage of the situation and began investing in some small start-up companies on the side. Even though I was fulfilling my responsibilities at Rheem and getting positive feedback from management, I should not have pursued personal business opportunities on company time, and I have since apologized to my contacts at Rheem for my behavior. I also have confessed it to the Lord.

While it is painful for me to make that admission—especially since I have tried to live my life with integrity in so many other ways—working side deals on company time was a blind spot for me. While I would like to avoid telling you about such a glaring flaw, this period is a crucial part of my story, as you will see in the chapters that follow.

Before the thought ever crossed my mind to take an ownership interest in another company, I discovered a resource that not only broadened my horizons and changed my way of thinking about business, but also literally changed my life.

Turning Point

As I moved from job to job during this period in my career, I learned that it pays to be observant of people and processes, and that it's important to take note of little details as well as the big issues.

There are common denominators among manufacturing companies, regardless of what they produce. All have functions such as receiving, shipping, quality control, and management. Through countless visits to distribution facilities and dealership operations, I started to see some of the same things—good and bad—happening in all of these places. Like Yogi Berra once quipped, "It's déjà vu all over again." For example, there are two seemingly insignificant yet very revealing signs of how a company treats its employees: the level of water pressure in drinking fountains and the cleanliness of rest rooms. When I visit a plant, two of the first things I do are to take a drink out of the nearest fountain and visit the men's room. I can learn a lot about how well the plant is managed and how much management cares about its workers before asking a single question.

I also have discovered that whether employees work in management or on the assembly line, I can learn a great deal by simply listening to them. The knowledge which can be gained from the employees themselves, sometimes referred to as "tribal knowledge," has proven to be extremely valuable.

This knowledge of company similarities and my personal observations give me confidence today when I walk into a manufacturing plant. Whether touring a simple sheet-metal shop or a major product manufacturer, I know what to look for. I've been in hundreds of plants in the USA and around the world, and I feel at home there because each job I've had along the way taught me valuable lessons about who and what it takes to make these plants operate day in and day out.

5

Turning to
The Wall Street Journal

One day during my first year at Rheem, I heard that our company had been acquired by a private equity group called KKR for about $400 million in cash. Previously, Rheem had been owned by City Investing in New York City.

The mergers and acquisitions (M&A) world was foreign to me and many of my associates. I didn't understand how M&A's work, nor did I understand the implications for Rheem employees who were now suddenly employed by a new owner.

Although I didn't have a clue about the intricate financial structures that may have been used for KKR to acquire Rheem, I was fascinated by the concept of one company buying another. The news immediately set my mind spinning with questions.

I recalled hearing on the nightly news about one large company buying another or buying a business going bankrupt. I knew the people doing these deals must be well educated and financially independent. Although I possessed neither formal education nor financial independence, that didn't stop me from dreaming. Something about this aspect of business made the hairs on my neck tingle with excitement.

"Who just acquired Rheem, and how does all this work?" I asked a colleague, wondering what changes the new ownership would bring about.

His answer was simple and direct: "If you want to understand the world of mergers and acquisitions, you need to read *The Wall Street Journal.*"

You may find this hard to believe, but at that point in my career I had never even heard of it. When my associate told me this was what I needed to read, I went to the local library and asked the librarian where I could find this "book." With a look of disbelief, she explained that *The Wall Street Journal* is a newspaper and that I needed to go to a newsstand to buy a copy. More than a little embarrassed, I left to find the nearest newsstand, purchased a copy, and headed home to read it. Little did I know I was about to embark on a new chapter in my life.

Published five days a week at the time (a Saturday edition was added later), *The Journal* was an escape for me into another world. Reading each issue from front to back took about three-and-a-half hours each day, but I fondly remember reading every article. When I first started, probably 40 percent was totally foreign to me, but I stayed with my study and for years I read *The Journal* every day from cover to cover. Nearly all the articles had financial terms and business explanations that were, at best, unfamiliar and in many cases, way over my head. As I kept reading, though, I was intrigued to discover the many possible methods by which one business could acquire another. And it was fascinating to ponder the orchestration of financial arrangements that made complicated transactions work.

My perseverance paid off because eventually, an unfamiliar word, strategy, or concept mentioned in one article would be explained in another I read in the days, weeks, and months that followed. For the first time in my life, I had discovered a resource that captivated me beyond anything else to which I had been exposed.

Patton Principle

17

Learning something new takes time, but it's time well spent. New knowledge can be life-changing. Even if it doesn't come quickly, stay with your plan to increase your understanding, and the long-term pay-off will likely be far greater than you expect.

Beyond mergers and acquisitions, *The Journal* was an eye-opening gateway to the business world at large. It not only exposed me to many other industries, but also to the practical, day-to-day problems businesses face. I learned about problems and solutions on a scale I could not experience first hand. Lacking any formal education in business—or even a college degree—left me with a huge gap in my understanding of the business world, but now I had something to help bridge the gulf between me and where I wanted to go someday.

The Journal was especially valuable in the way strategic reasoning was described in detail. The newspaper also followed some stories over an extended period of time, many of which read like chapters in a novel. The people featured in these articles seemed fairytale-like to me. I couldn't help but wonder about their personal lives and families and the educational backgrounds which enabled them to successfully complete high-level acquisitions and divestures.

While I was learning many valuable on-the-job lessons at Rheem, *The Journal* became my print mentor for the larger business world, and it kept me current on the latest financial news. I always had an eye out for stories about the heating and air conditioning industry, and over the years I found opportunities to discuss current articles with my colleagues. My up-to-date knowledge of our industry often made me look a lot smarter than I was and elevated me in the eyes of my distributors as well as their customers.

Patton Principle

18

Educate thyself. It's tempting to think school is the answer for anyone who really wants an education. The truth is, if you find something you seriously need or want to know, there are countless resources that will teach you. Find them. Use them. Let your passion for knowledge drive you.

While I was mesmerized by what I read, I still never dreamed *The Wall Street Journal* would provide me with the business education I needed to one day launch an international career of restructuring manufacturing companies, eventually totaling billions of dollars in revenue. There would be many intermediate steps along the way, but all were part of educating me to reach the next level of my career.

My self-education lacked the structured, sequential approach of a formal business program, but over the years I acquired valuable knowledge that helped me think conceptually and systematically about mergers and acquisitions. Eventually, I became completely comfortable discussing business deals. I also grew to understand the complex financial side of businesses, including balance sheets, cash flow statements, and profit and loss statements.

The significance of what I'd learned was reinforced in January 2007 when I received an e-mail from Mark Campbell, marketing and sales director for *The Wall Street Journal*. Mark explained that the publisher read an article about me in a business publication in which I mentioned how helpful The Journal had been in my career, and he passed the information along to Mark.

Mark was working on a project to introduce young executives to the benefits of *The Wall Street Journal*, focusing particularly on how staying informed through the paper and its Web site would help them get ahead in their developing careers. His e-mail asked if I would provide a testimonial for *The Journal's* marketing materials.

Wow. I was honored by the request and gave him the following testimonial for the publication that has been so influential in my life:

> I developed an interest in mergers and acquisitions after a company I worked for was purchased by a competitor. I didn't understand how an acquisition worked, and a co-worker I questioned about the process suggested I start reading *The Wall Street Journal*.... Now, twenty-five years later, as founder and senior managing partner for a private equity firm, I continue to rely on *The Journal* for relevant news and business trends.

When I started reading *The Wall Street Journal* in 1981, I never would have guessed I would one day be quoted in its marketing materials about how the paper helped me achieve a successful career. But then, I never could have imagined the career God had in store for me, or that one day I would be doing "Wall Street Journal" deals with companies around the world.

Patton Principle

19

Just when you think you've got it all figured out, remember you don't. There's no such thing as a true know-it-all, so always be open to learning more, no matter how much you already know. Even if you have it all figured out, God has more in store than you can imagine.

The downside of my "program" was that the education derived from a book, newspaper, or teacher could take me only so far. Some knowledge must be acquired by working in "live" business situations, such as revenue forecasting and annual budgeting. As I ventured out on my first few deals (more about that in the next two chapters), I learned some painful but necessary lessons. While I understood financial terminology after years of reading *The Journal,* I didn't always understand how to apply my knowledge correctly, nor did I realize the implications of some of my decisions—until it was too late.

Financial advisor Dave Ramsey describes financial mistakes as a "stupid tax." While I've certainly paid my share of those taxes, I believe the real tragedy comes from not learning from mistakes and either repeating them or becoming discouraged and giving up on one's dreams. I chose to learn from my mistakes and now consider them to be investments which helped me attain a successful business career and financial freedom.

Walt Disney pointed out that "all your dreams can come true if you have the courage to pursue them."

But as he also noted, and as I was about to learn firsthand, "It takes a lot of money to make those dreams come true."

Turning Point

Call me dumb or call me lucky, but discovering *The Wall Street Journal* when I did wasn't dumb luck, it was Divine Providence.

They say a blind squirrel finds an acorn every now and then, but like all the other turning points in my life, learning about *The Journal* was no accident. For those who follow the Lord, there are no "coincidences." After buying that first *Journal* issue, I have read it every day, and I believe God brought this crucial resource to my attention so I could benefit from the wealth of information it contains and help complete my business education in preparation for my long-term career. And by the way, there's another much-needed resource that I read every day: The Bible, God's Word. For wisdom in business—and every area of life—it is unmatched. For preparation for life long term, and I mean really long term (eternal), it is a necessity.

Turning Deals but Not Profits

As I visited Ruud distributors in my region, I noticed a pattern: Whenever a distributor's sales rep would take me to one of his HVAC contractor customers, I saw paperwork scattered around the office in what looked like disorganized piles. The larger the contractor, the bigger the piles seemed to be.

As with most small businesses at the time, these contractors didn't have a computer and did their accounting manually. I saw a need for contractors to have a computerized accounting system that would manage accounting functions such as payroll, general ledger, and accounts receivable, yet most of them could not afford to buy a computer.

My glimmer of opportunity to do something with my observation happened one day when I ran across an advertisement from a company offering computer system time-sharing. The ad targeted entrepreneurs who would duplicate the company's business model in different geographic regions. Intrigued by the concept and the potential it had for air conditioning contractors, I arranged to visit the company's office in Chicago.

Without any knowledge whatsoever about computers or the software that ran them, I was ready to jump at this business opportunity. I was convinced computer time-sharing could be the thriving business opportunity of a lifetime—even though I had not done any research about existing competition or a comparative analysis of the cost to own a computer versus "renting" time to use one. In truth, there were many critical questions that should have been answered before taking the next step, but I was blinded by optimism and couldn't wait to get started.

My version of the business model was to provide contractors a way to time-share a computer for an average monthly fee of six hundred dollars. The company selling the concept didn't mention that I would need a computer programmer to write and modify programs, but it probably wouldn't have mattered since I didn't know the difference between hardware and software.

At an air conditioning industry meeting a year earlier, I had heard a guest speaker named Carl Parker who had more than twenty-five years of industry experience and at one time was a highly profitable HVAC distributor in middle Tennessee. I approached Carl about the time-sharing concept for HVAC contractors, and he immediately liked the idea. Although he was capable of underwriting the start-up cost of about fifty thousand dollars, he saw the wisdom of my "having skin in the game," so we each invested 50 percent in the company and called our operation The Computer Connection. With his extensive contacts, Carl procured our first two customers: a residential HVAC distributor and a commercial HVAC contractor. The revenue they generated nearly paid our monthly expenses, but there was no money left over for Carl and me at the end of the month.

In those days, computers were fairly new—and very big. We rented an office to house the computer, which was the size of two dishwashers. With one 1200 baud modem, it was far beyond what any of the contractors had at the time, and for their monthly fee, our customers had access to the computer for two hours a day. To access the system, the contractors needed a modem to interface with ours, a terminal screen, and commercial-grade printer, which they purchased from us. Customers would log on remotely and update their accounts payables, accounts receivables, job costing, invoicing, and payroll. The software was interfaced within all these programs and saved the contractor time and money—at least that was how it was supposed to work.

When I purchased the computer and software, the seller in Illinois assured me the system was integrated so everything would work together seamlessly. But I found out the hard way that wasn't exactly the case. When our first customer entered data, the entries didn't carry over to the next column, and that glitch was just the beginning of our problems with the software. It turned out to be defective in a number of areas and would cause the computer to crash. Before long, I was wondering what I'd gotten myself into.

When I raised these issues with the owner of the company from which I purchased the system, he acknowledged there were some problems but didn't do anything to resolve them. Carl and I were faced with the choice of suing his company or hiring a programmer to de-bug the software. We chose the latter, and it decimated our monthly budget.

In addition to the software programmer, I also hired a person to train customers to operate the computer and organize various accounting functions, while I focused on sales and marketing. Theresa became the office manager, and within the first year and a half, we had fifteen customers signed up, including an elevator installer, nursing home, floral shop, and numerous construction contractors. To handle the additional volume, we upgraded from a single telephone line to a multiplexer equivalent to twenty or so individual phone lines.

As our customer base increased, so did the expenses necessary to support them. I generated enough revenue to pay my employees and our office expenses each month, but not Carl or me. This became a frustrating pattern, and I couldn't understand why we were always running out of money (it was mainly my frustration—Carl had already owned an extremely profitable company and received the fruits of his labor). I considered myself a good money manager, and my personal credit was impeccable. The computer business, however, was in a different league than merely reconciling my personal checkbook each month.

I didn't understand the relationship between the profit and loss statement and the balance sheet, a limitation which only added to my frustrations. The Computer Connection's books were maintained on the computer system, and our accountant prepared the company's tax returns. I complained to him once about our lack of cash, and his response just made me mad. He talked about cash flow and the need for working capital, but I didn't have another cent to put into the business.

One day our accountant told me a tax bill was due, and I had no money to pay it. That was the last straw. We sold the business to an installer of DEC computer systems who wanted to convert our customer base to his own stand-alone computer systems and then provide long-term support. That solved my cash flow problem, but after more than two years in the business, I hadn't made a penny for all my efforts!

Because I didn't do my due diligence, I also missed spotting competition just around the corner—the personal computer. Our minimum monthly time-share fee was six hundred dollars, which could increase if, for instance, a larger customer required additional disc storage space. Extra training also cost more. One customer paid twelve hundred dollars a month primarily because of re-training expenses. By comparison at the time, a personal computer cost about five thousand dollars, and a printer and modem were about a thousand dollars each. So at the end of one year of time-sharing, many of our clients could have purchased their own systems and paid them off.

Patton Principle

20

Be optimistic but realistic. You may be onto a great idea, but before you jump in, check out all the pitfalls. Optimism, inspiration, motivation, and attitude will help you keep going. Just be sure you're on a path worth going on—and that it's not a dead end.

Even though I made no monetary profit from my computer venture, I did learn some valuable lessons from co-owning the business. I saw what it takes to run a small business with just three employees, while serving as a part-time salesman. I discovered the importance of due diligence and the need to understand what the marketplace wants before starting an uphill climb that at the end of the day was not worth the effort. I also experienced the stress of having a bank loan with my personal guarantee. My favorable credit has always been a big asset and having it at risk was hard on my wife-to-be and me.

Shortly after selling The Computer Connection, a mutual friend introduced me to a man named Michael, who soon became my partner in a second venture. Michael had experience in the video rental business, an industry then in the early stages of the home video boom. In readymade, day-to-day grocery store traffic, he saw a video rental opportunity that most were missing. To capitalize on this hole in the market, he created a business model that provided a computerized system for renting videos to these stores so they, in turn, could rent them to their customers.

Michael had terrible credit (which should have been an early warning sign to me), so I provided the financing through a combination of debt and equity, including, once again, a bank loan with my personal guarantee. He handled the operational duties and marketing, but we didn't form a legal business. Through a "gentlemen's agreement," we agreed to split profits fifty-fifty. Need I tell you this was a big mistake?

We offered about 150 videos for each store and included the hardware and software for tracking rentals, along with barcoding equipment and a point of sale display located near the grocery store's check-out area. Every week we rotated new videos into the stores, so customers continuously had new selections available. Each store received a cut of the gross revenues and had no involvement other than taking inventory of the videos and checking them in and out. Our bar coding greatly simplified this added task.

After the first few stores were up and running, we began expanding. Winn-Dixie saw what we were doing, and they approached us. We were impressed with ourselves for that easy victory and before long we were stocking videos in a major chain store. It was a joy to see a business idea go from paper to a live, up-and-running business making profits.

As our business and profits grew, Michael decided he no longer wanted to keep the same equity arrangements. He found another source for financing, paid off the bank debt, and terminated our gentleman's agreement. As a result, I made a fraction of what I could have if we had formed a corporation and issued equity positions. Having ownership in a legal entity that owns the inventory, cash, and other assets would have made it much more difficult for Michael to just walk away and start a new venture.

Over the years, I've learned there are two situations that reveal a person's true character in business: when he or she is in the bunker or when she or he experiences success. When things go wrong and the repercussions are costly, there is, of course, a great amount of stress. For instance, when the bank loan payment comes due on the fifteenth and there's no money to pay it, does your partner join in and look for sources, or does the partner point fingers and refuse to help? Fear is a common emotion, such as the fear of having to file for bankruptcy, and it's human nature to want to run away from danger when things get tough. Staying in the bunker to help save the business is the most important sign of real character in your partner.

At the other end of the spectrum is financial success. Greed can show its ugly face within a business partnership in a host of ways, ranging from misuse of one's expense report to theft, fraud, and outright lies. This can happen if the wealth is truly present in a profitable business or even when there's simply a great deal of cash generated, whether or not the month-end financials prove the company is genuinely performing well. Few things are more satisfying than a partnership that ends with the partners still feeling their friendship will last a lifetime.

Patton Principle

21

Gentlemen put their gentlemen's agreements in writing. Even if everyone means well, misunderstandings can happen, and crisis situations can make the best of us become our worst selves. So if everyone really means well, no one will mind having important agreements in writing.

You'd think I would have learned the importance of formal agreements between partners, but my next deal was also a gentlemen's agreement—this time with Dwayne, an established builder of upper-end "spec" (speculative) homes. Dwayne built houses in the $3 million range offering ten thousand square feet of living space, up to five car garages, on three to five level acres in a manicured sub-division. My part of the business was to arrange a construction loan with a commercial lender that included weekly draws as the work progressed on the home as well as an advance for overhead expenses. We agreed to split the profits evenly after the builder's overhead, real estate commissions, and other direct marketing expenses for each custom estate home.

So why would a builder turn to an individual like me to provide financing for a home? It has to do with how the financing and construction process work. A bank provides two services for construction loans. First, it supplies financing and second, it has a standard method of disbursing the loan to the contractor based on the percentage of work completed.

The bank divides home construction into increments of 1/2 percent to 5 percent. For instance, clearing the lot of debris and digging basic footers may account for 2 percent of the home's overall construction. Next in line may be purchasing the blocks and cement needed to build the foundation of the home. That incremental piece might be 4 percent. Later, installation of the roof shingles and completion of the fireplaces could be another 5 or 6 percent.

After a bank representative visits the site and verifies that a particular task or stage has indeed been completed, the bank deposits the prorated percentage of the construction loan into the contractor's account. This makes sure the builder doesn't receive more cash than the percentage of completion should allow. The bank's verification of progress and its control of the construction funds is also a benefit to the future homeowner, because the codes compliance built into the process ensures each step is done properly.

From the builder's perspective, however, the process limits the number of homes that can be built at any given time. Normally, a contractor borrows from the bank as much as his credit allows. Once he reaches capacity, he has to wait for one of his spec homes to sell before he can start the next one.

My financing (including my wife's agreement to proceed with this venture) allowed Dwayne to undertake an additional construction project. If he could build three homes based on his own credit, now he could do a fourth one with my help. As with a bank loan, he would get paid incrementally for his overhead, and we agreed to split the profits when the home sold.

My father had drilled into my head the importance of having good credit—a lesson I have imparted to my son as well—and I was able to get a bank loan for this project, because I had always kept my credit "clean." (Good credit is one of the most critical aspects of having a successful career as an entrepreneur.) To demonstrate the soundness of our plans to the bank, Dwayne and I stressed that he was a reputable builder and that the price range was comparable to his previous projects. Armed with a proposed floor plan and elevations of what the houses would look like, we described Dwayne's experience and showed how the house would complement the subdivision. We then presented a detailed cost analysis, by stages of construction.

Our proposal also included the value of the completed house, based on comps, an overhead allocation for Dwayne to pay expenses, and our agreed-upon fifty-fifty profit split. The collateral was the home and land, the imbedded profit of the job, and my personal guarantee—which included my own home, cars, investments, and anything else I owned.

While the bank had its in-house attorney and standard construction contract to cover all major issues, Dwayne and I had a separate gentlemen's agreement to include me in the profits of other homes he built in the subdivision for which I provided financing. After I secured the loan, Dwayne started building the house and to everyone's delight sold it during the framing stages, just one month into a six-month construction timeline. But Dwayne went back on his word and never used me again for the fifteen or so additional houses he built in that subdivision. When I asked why he cut me out of those projects, he told me he thought our arrangement was unfair to him, and he felt justified reneging on our agreement.

Although I walked away with some profit from the one deal (my portion was about $40,000 on a house that sold for more than $2 million), I would have realized much greater profits had I insisted our agreement be spelled out in a formal contract so Dwayne would have been forced to uphold his side of the deal when it came to building additional homes in that sub-division.

In addition to recognizing the need for a formal agreement for every business transaction regardless of size, I learned something from this experience that was substantiated by some of my later deals: If you negotiate too good a deal for yourself, it will come back to haunt you. Over the life of a deal, the partnership arrangement has to be fair to both parties. Otherwise, in the months or years to follow, the participants will think back on how the deal was set up, who said what, and who did what to influence the final equity structure. If it is weighted too favorably to one side, someone is not going to be happy, and the final results won't be, either. From my experience with Dwayne, I learned to think ahead about how both sides would fare and make sure that the parties would look back and say they would have done the same deal again.

In the new home construction business with Dwayne, I could see his point about our deal being unfair to him because it didn't have an ending point (until the entire development was finished—about five hundred building lots). By using revolving credit, I would earn half of his net profits on each house I financed, which really was too good a deal for me because, other than financial exposure, I didn't have to do anything.

But it was wrong for him to go back on his word. I would have been open to working out a compromise, such as limiting the number of homes to four. It was unfair that I was only able to participate in one deal, especially after the risk I had assumed on his behalf. My short-lived construction financing business was yet another lesson learned the hard way.

Patton Principle 22

Win-win situations are the only way to win. Fair is fair. Make sure each deal has adequate provisions for everyone involved to benefit. If you get more than your share, it may fill your bank account, but it will leave your relationships empty and unhappy.

My next venture turned out much better. After a tanning session one day, Theresa came home with the idea of opening her own tanning spa. At the time when Theresa first discovered this new-born industry, tanning salons typically were located in retail space at a strip mall, usually near a hair salon, but the one Theresa patronized was about thirty miles north of our home.

After some due-diligence (Theresa was smarter than I when it came to checking out the competition), she could not find an exclusive tanning spa in Nashville, only a tanning bed here or there in a beauty salon. She realized we could own the first one in all of Nashville, Tennessee.

At the time, a tanning bed cost about $7,500 and a salon could have six or more beds, so the upfront costs weren't cheap. Customers paid eight dollars for a salon visit that lasted twenty to thirty minutes, with discounts available if multiple visits were purchased in advance. The salon could be run by two employees and a manager or owner, so labor costs were not especially high, but the hours were long.

A friend of mine named Mike and I put together equity financing for the initial investment of $50,000, which included working capital and six beds. As with previous deals, the profits were split evenly. We had to build out the leased space for our store, which we called Riviera Tanning Spa. We took advantage of the landlord's build-out allowance, a common practice for new tenants. The amount of money a landlord provides a tenant to get the space ready for opening typically is based on the amount of square footage leased—the more square feet rented, the more money available. The length of the lease and the type of enterprise going into the space also are taken into consideration.

Theresa was the boss from day one. She made the hiring and firing decisions and handled all the day-to-day operations. Our first month's gross revenue was a stunning $30,000. It was an awesome feeling to have such great success, especially since Mike and I were essentially just the bankers, and Theresa did the real work! Before long, we opened a second spa in Nashville, and the money began to roll in—as did competition. The hair salon next to our first location noticed our success and installed tanning beds in its store. Not only did we begin experiencing lower revenues, but also lower margins.

When Theresa became pregnant, we decided to let one lease expire, and we sold the other to a competitor. By that time, the price per visit had dropped to only four dollars, and although we were in the tanning business less than three years, we made very good money, especially before competition grew. Theresa is an excellent businesswoman, and the only credit I can take is having been smart enough to invest in her enterprise.

Patton Principle 23

Know when to quit—and quit. Except for heaven, good things don't last forever. So as long as you're doing business on this earth, stay vigilant to know when you've achieved all you can from a given opportunity. Moving on to the next good thing keeps your business fresh and profitable.

Unfortunately, my next venture didn't turn out nearly as well. After our salon business success, I was looking for another project and ran across a business-opportunity advertisement from a company called Comfort Seal. The Ohio-based company installed waterproof rubber roofs for mobile homes.

Having previously lived in a mobile home, I was well aware that their roofs could begin to rattle as they aged, and the noise was a major nuisance. The Comfort Seal material prevented roof leaks, and as an added benefit, prevented rattling. (The worn-out tires you sometimes see anchored to mobile home roofs solve the same noise problem.)

Comfort Seal's mobile home roof also used hard-board insulation underneath the rubber membrane, which could be trimmed to the necessary size. The long sheets of rubber came in ten, fifteen, and twenty-foot widths and were permanently sealed to each other with a patented s-shaped interlocking system.

Intrigued by this concept, I took a trip to Ohio to learn more. The operations there consisted of a small office, a call center for telemarketing, a dock for installation crews, and a storage area for the roofing materials. The owner and I visited a large mobile home park where the Comfort Seal roofing had been in place on some of the homes for several years, and the residents were pleased with the results. We also visited a few other mobile home sites in the same park where the Comfort Seal system was being installed, so I observed firsthand how the insulation barrier and rubber membrane were affixed to the existing structure before being covered by the rubber roofing.

The owner had no substantial plan for expanding his business—just a hope, a dream, and a good product concept. He planned to charge someone like me a one-time fee to learn how to install his roofing system and to acquire the contacts needed for purchasing materials.

I was hooked by what I heard and saw and decided to invest in the business by duplicating the process in Tennessee. Without any further due diligence (a big mistake—again), I formed an S Corporation for tax reasons and for protection in case of a lawsuit from an unhappy mobile home owner. With a bank loan to match my equity of $35,000, I rented space for a phone system to use for telemarketing mobile home owners within a hundred-mile radius. Rubber roofs worked for 90 percent of the mobile homes on the market, so the potential seemed great to me.

My real vision, however, was to work with rubber manufacturers and create a national distribution network to sell to local dealerships. My idea also included pre-cutting the rubber sheets into a handful of sizes to be trimmed out at the final job site. Included in the kit would be the insulation boards, rolls of duct tape, the correct number and size of screws for each phase of the job, and a video to demonstrate the installation technique.

I paid to have a video produced showing the installation process and also hired a writer to put together an instruction manual (my Roper experience with the mysterious metal shavings "burned" into my memory the importance of instructions, and I decided not to neglect that critical element in my own business). It helped that the installation itself was not especially difficult, and there was nothing else on the market like this roofing system. By providing volume discounts and steady business, everyone would benefit.

It all sounded good, but I never was able to pull it off. In just a year and a half, we ran out of mobile home owners within a two hundred mile radius. That meant our serviceable distance was almost twice as far as I originally planned, and sales began to slow significantly as a result.

Less than two years after starting Comfort Seal in Tennessee, I realized it was a losing cause. The dealer concept never reached a sufficient volume to interest the manufacturer in supplying rubber pre-cut to our specifications. So after paying the bank loan and expenses, I lost about $40,000.

As became painfully evident in hindsight, due diligence is a critical step in any deal. Although I found one source that cited the number of existing mobile homes in middle Tennessee by county, the information turned out to be inaccurate. I should have validated the market statistics through more than one source, but I took the numbers at face value.

When I ran out of mobile home owners in middle Tennessee, I faced the prospect of expanding my geographical footprint much farther than I originally anticipated. The expense of traveling longer distances to install mobile home roofs created problems in our cost structure.

Had I done proper due diligence, I likely also would have discovered that one of the reasons Comfort Seal worked well in Ohio was because that area had more mobile homes than Tennessee. Although the owner of Comfort Seal was from Indiana, he started his roofing business in Ohio because of the large market there. In addition, the customer base in Ohio was different because compared to people in Tennessee, they tended to be more interested in long-term mobile home living and putting money into improvements. Finally, mobile home owners in Ohio were more capable of paying for the rubber roofs.

I added another uphill battle by attempting to create a nationwide system, so my start-up costs were much higher than they would have been for a single outlet. If I had focused instead on getting well established in middle Tennessee, I would have seen early on that I didn't have the capacity to go national anytime soon.

My business plan lacked the insight of factoring in appropriate start-up expenses. In addition, I should have gone beyond scratching the surface to make sure I truly understood the potential market in terms of size, interest, and financial capacity for my product. And as with any start-up, there was no financial background to review for a picture of what to expect. Without historical financials, there is no way to compare previous numbers to current numbers, and over the years I've avoided getting involved with start-up companies for that singular reason.

I have held business ownership positions in a number of other companies as well, but these represent the diverse industries in which I have dabbled and the mistakes I made along the way. I have often wondered if a college education would have taught me these lessons in the classroom instead of my learning them the hard way. But Theresa, a college graduate herself, assures me college would only have educated me to a certain level. The real lessons usually were gained through on-the-job training and the school of hard knocks.

Even my *Wall Street Journal* "education" could take me only so far. As helpful as *The Journal* was, owning a business provides a litany of experiences that is impossible to get even by reading all the newspapers in the world. One simply cannot learn everything from a classroom setting, textbooks, newspapers, and magazines.

Operating solely from book knowledge is akin to learning to swim on land. You can go through the motions, but at some point you have to get in the water. In my case, lack of understanding about the standard reporting methods of the profit and loss statement, balance sheet, and cash flow statement was a serious stumbling block on the operational side.

Anyone in a similar situation would have the same problem. The key to understanding a business is the historical financial data the business has generated. A proper understanding of this vital information is critical to business valuation and the cash requirements for daily operations.

The biggest mistakes I made were directly linked to not fully understanding the financials and my lack of sophistication in recognizing how they work together to provide a comprehensive picture of a business. Financials are the lifeblood of every operation, and understanding them is absolutely imperative to success.

As much as I had learned, my world of small business transactions was still too little to satisfy my dreams. My deals didn't feel nearly as significant as the deals I read about on Wall Street. Even though I was on my way up the "deal ladder", I couldn't wait to get further. I truly believed I could be as successful as some of the businessmen and women routinely profiled in *The Journal.* I longed for an opportunity to prove myself in the big leagues and began making plans to find an opportunity that would allow me to work full time running my own company.

It became my dream—and obsession.

Turning Point

I thought a good idea alone was a guarantee of success but came to realize that the devil is in the details—especially the financial statements.

From the nature of my agreements to the amount of due diligence to the numbers on a spreadsheet, the lesson was the same: to overlook small things in planning will cause big problems later on. The Bible says that "the inexperienced believe anything, but the sensible watch their steps" (Proverbs 14:15). In many respects, I was inexperienced but gained some much needed business sense during this time. Through all the twists and turns in these smaller ventures, I emerged with a better understanding of what it takes to run a business. I also developed a yearning to go to the next level and do a bigger deal. I was weary of making small profits and

---

sometimes, no profits at all. Deep down, what I most wanted was to be owner of a profitable stand-alone business that generated enough cash flow and profit to allow me to take a salary. I was motivated by my need to be successful financially and to be recognized as such by my peers. I didn't realize I was about to take a different turn—different like driving down a country road is different from cruising the interstate.

Turn, Baby, Turn

7

After eight years of learning about mergers and acquisitions by reading *The Wall Street Journal* and dabbling part time in the ownership of several small businesses, I began looking for an acquisition that would allow me to quit my job at Rheem and work full time in my own business. I thought I was finally ready to take on a greater challenge and fulfill my dream of running a manufacturing company. And I knew exactly what product I wanted to make.

While still working for Rheem, I formed a partnership with Troy, a fellow Tennessean, to sell Quonset buildings. Quonset huts, as they're also called, are lightweight, rounded, prefabricated metal-roof structures commonly used for storage. They are much cheaper than traditionally constructed outbuildings, and the profit margin on them is very favorable.

Troy, one of the best salesmen I've ever met, was importing Quonset buildings from a Canadian manufacturer. The problem with that arrangement was that we had to pay a high tariff as well as the cost of middle men who distributed the huts. I saw this as an opportunity to increase our profit by cutting out the middle men—the manufacturers and their sales representatives—and avoid paying tariffs by finding a U.S. manufacturer to make Quonset buildings for us.

I had only $10,000 from my previous business deals to invest in a new venture, which of course was not enough to think seriously about acquiring a manufacturer. Still, that didn't stop me from dreaming big.

Given my modest working capital, I realized the more realistic approach was to establish a relationship with a manufacturer and, as the money began rolling in (assuming I could structure a sweetheart deal that way), transition to becoming the dominant owner.

While my initial search included the entire United States, I hoped to find a manufacturer near middle Tennessee because of the high costs of freight to transport the buildings. I also wanted to stay within the Rheem marketing area for which I was responsible and not travel any more than necessary. This, of course, was before the Internet was available to help me with my search, so I began with a trip to the library to look up Standard Industry Classification (SIC) codes. I was excited to find just what I wanted in Nashville, not far from my home.

Mid-South was a company that could perform all the functions necessary to manufacture Quonset buildings. It was located in an older section of town "on the wrong side of the tracks," as most of my friends and confidants commented, and had roots in the Industrial Revolution. Although Mid-South had been a manufacturing powerhouse in the early 1960s, now in 1986, the company was well past its prime. Nevertheless, Mid-South's versatility and convenient location made it an ideal place to manufacture Quonset buildings, and I decided to pay a visit.

The Mid-South plant covered an entire city block, with the front entrance facing the street. On a parallel street, there was an exit where final goods were loaded for transportation. As I drove by, neither side provided a good view or any indication of the capabilities inside. Overgrown trees, shrubs, weeds, and perennials created a setting more like an African safari camp than a manufacturing plant.

When I entered the back parking lot, the size of Mid-South's facilities became clear. The tool and die shop alone was about a hundred yards long. Yet, there were only two cars in the pothole-filled parking lot. This struck me as odd because I was there on a weekday during business hours. The complex consisted of three buildings: an office/showroom, the tool and die job shop, and a stamping building. Together, they provided about fifty thousand square feet of space, but all three looked to have been in a state of neglect for a decade or more. It was obvious no one had done any work to their exteriors in a long time.

The day after my drive-by, I called the office and spoke with the owner's daughter. As we talked, I heard cats meowing in the background, which perhaps was an omen of the lion's den I was about to step into. I later learned that she loved cats and seemed to have one around every corner of the stale, out-dated showroom, Engineering Department, and Administrative Support Office.

After briefly introducing myself, I explained I was looking for a manufacturing facility to make a product and thought Mid-South might fit the bill perfectly. What activities, I inquired, was Mid-South currently involved with?

"There's little to no activity here," she replied nonchalantly, "and that's how my father likes it."

I asked if I could make an appointment to visit and meet Clayton, the owner, to learn more about Mid-South's capabilities.

She assured me that no appointment was necessary as Clayton came in around 9 o'clock each morning and stayed for two or three hours almost every business day of the year.

I was curious. What type of owner shunned activity in his company? It didn't take me long to find out. As I entered the tool and die shop, the place looked even worse inside than out. It was difficult to see much because only three fluorescent lights were working in the entire building. Fortunately, a little light came in from the open bay and side doors. Otherwise, I would have been reluctant to enter that dark cavern!

I later toured the press shop building and discovered the roof had large holes in it, exposing the shop to whatever weather happened along. All three buildings were in desperate need of maintenance, and I suspect most people would have said, "Just raze it and start over."

In its 1960s heyday, Mid-South employed about 350 people. Sadly, Clayton and his former partner, now deceased, had allowed this once thriving manufacturing plant to go downhill to the point where I couldn't believe the place was even usable under current Occupational Safety and Health Administration (OSHA) standards, let alone capable of manufacturing or fabricating anything of value or in real volume.

There were only three employees in the press shop, and it was clear from the unpleasant eye they gave me as I walked casually past the receiving bay doors that they didn't like having visitors. The press shop featured a worn-out couch that two of the three employees used for break time and naps. To add to the dismal environment, Clayton didn't allow air conditioning or heat to be turned on, so the workers were always either hot or cold.

As if this were not enough, twenty or so years prior, a union tried unsuccessfully to organize the employee base at Mid-South, and in the process, union members sabotaged and booby trapped the electrical wiring of almost every piece of equipment before the workers were physically removed by the police. The sabotaged wiring easily could have killed someone.

The owners' response to the attempts to unionize the plant was to close the place down and go to Florida for six months. This, of course, stranded the customer base with all their orders incomplete. It also quickly scattered both the skilled and unskilled labor force over a three-state area rich with tool and die work during a period of national economic growth.

The strategy used to defeat the union worked, but the company never operated again in a meaningful way. As the saying goes, the operation was a success, but the patient died.

Now, Clayton was the sole owner, and he continued to pace the floors of the tool and die shop—a shell of its former self—just as he had done in its glory days. I later learned that he rarely went in the press shop and never went into the office or showroom area. Perhaps he avoided the showroom because it was infested with spiders and roaming cats, or maybe it was because the place reminded him too much of his real love: the engineering aspect of producing metal parts in shapes and configurations only a true artist could appreciate.

As I looked around at the remnants of this once magnificent facility, it was immediately apparent I could never bring a potential customer in for a plant tour, even though visits were almost always required prior to work being contracted out. The plant was a dilapidated job-shop with dated presses, grinders, planers, lathes, and other heavy duty equipment to form hard steel, aluminum, and other metals into all shapes and dimensions. The place was filthy, a truly depressing sight for anyone who understood and loved the manufacturing industry. The legacy of Mid-South and companies like it was to be the first to get involved with new products, and every tool and die shop was special to those of us who love manufacturing.

To make Mid-South competitive again clearly would require expensive and time-consuming renovations, including updating the equipment to fulfill contemporary tolerances of thousandths of an inch. Despite these impediments, I immediately began thinking about how I could buy the place.

24

Find possibilities where others see none. Having a vision allows you to see what could happen while most people see only problems. If you temper your creative energies with critical thinking (due diligence!), you stand to succeed where no one else will even try. "Chance" does favor the prepared mind.

In the dim glow of the tool and die shop's three florescent lights, I saw the owner bending over one of the shop's many grinders, holding a metal part in his hand. In his mid-60s, he was about six feet tall, trim, and obviously in command. He barked orders to the only employee in the place.

I called from a distance so as not to startle him, "My name is Jim Patton. Can I talk with you for a few minutes?"

He turned indifferently to eyeball me a little better and nodded. He was not the least bit impressed with another visitor.

It soon became apparent he enjoyed conversation with someone knowledgeable about the manufacturing business. I learned that he was producing a few products for a couple of friends, but I was much more impressed with the fact he produced replacement parts for the automotive after-market that required some fairly tight tolerances. His customer, M & M, was based about a hundred miles north in Kentucky.

As I explained the purpose of my visit, Clayton made it clear he wasn't interested in gearing up the facility to make Quonset buildings in the quality and volume I needed. In a low scratchy voice, with not a single machine running in the entire plant, he dismissed my idea.

"Had a guy in here just last week wanting me to gear up for his baseball batting cages, too. Gave him the same answer as you—no thanks."

I asked if he would mind my coming back again because I could see the impressive strength this place possessed to bend, cut, or shape metals. Mid-South's potential captured my imagination, and I envisioned a time when it could be fully operational once again. If I didn't know before that visit, I knew it now: manufacturing was in my blood all right, and the thought of Mid-South rising from the ashes to become a dynamic manufacturing plant lured me irresistibly. I decided, then and there, that I had to pursue this challenge at all costs. Little did I know just how extreme those costs would turn out to be.

I'd like to return with a proposal to buy Mid-South," I said, having no idea where I would come up with the money.

He nodded his head offhandedly, as if he had heard that line before, too. Still, his nod indicated he would allow me to come back, which let me know that, at the very least, he liked me a little bit and maybe even accepted me as one that shared his love for manufacturing.

His daughter later confirmed that Clayton did, in fact, like me, explaining that more visitors had been thrown out of his place than were allowed to stay during the last decade or so. She knew the pattern well, since her father asked her to answer the phone calls he didn't want in the first place.

The owner didn't care about inquiries from business people, nor did he want Mid-South to produce much of anything. Could it be he just lacked the energy and desire to resurrect Mid-South? Whatever the reason he didn't want to rebuild the business, he still couldn't bring himself to just close the doors for good. I remember thinking I could win him over if I found a way to bring Mid-South back to life while allowing him to continue roaming the aisles with no stress or real responsibility.

After several more visits over the following weeks, I became enamored with the place and set my mind to purchase the facility and make it viable again. Clayton even allowed a smile or two during a conversation when he described with his hands as much with words about the manufacturing he had done in years gone by. I saw a twinkle in the old man's eyes as I described to him how the place could be cranked back up without any investment on his part and, more importantly, no employee headaches. He made it clear to me that the revival would be my sole responsibility since he didn't want a bunch of know-it-all bankers crawling all over his equipment.

"Bankers don't know how to run a real company. They only-structure loans so tight they would choke a horse." He obviously knew the dark side of a commercial bank loan, too.

Through an old acquaintance, I found four silent partners to put up funding in exchange for ownership in the company. My equity was only 20 percent initially, but there were built-in incentives for me to become a majority holder in the distant future. Meanwhile, at my request, one of the partners with commercial real estate experience came over to take a look around Mid-South as part of my early, "slow drive-by" due diligence.

"Jim, is that an actual hole in the press room's roof?" he asked in shock.

Compared to his newly constructed commercial shopping centers, Mid-South must have been quite a sight to him.

"You could literally drop a Volkswagen through the roof and nothing would touch the car as it fell," he said with irony—and without stretching the truth.

One of the holes in the roof was huge, and it was clear that the amount of work needed to make Mid-South respectable was staggering. I had to do some hard selling to get this potential partner to believe in me and commit cash to the deal I was putting together. But in the end, he decided to invest in the venture.

While this informal due diligence was in progress, Clayton gave me a detailed list of equipment from an appraisal that had been done ten or fifteen years prior. It provided a thorough account of Mid-South's equipment and individualized capabilities. Even someone not familiar with manufacturing would be impressed with the company's extensive resources. It became clear to me that with these assets and Mid-South's strategic position in the southeastern United States, the business could return to the level of work that once required hundreds of employees.

The bank wanted an updated appraisal of Mid-South, which is standard practice prior to a purchase of this nature. However, when I contacted the company that did the original appraisal to see about getting an updated version, I discovered to my dismay that it had gone out of business. An entirely new appraisal would cost twenty-five to fifty thousand dollars, a dramatic increase in the cost of my due diligence, so I tried taking a short cut by looking for an appraiser who would accept the old appraisal and revalue it.

I didn't realize it then, but few appraisal companies will accept another party's appraisal, one reason being that it would be detrimental to their overall profit strategy. It's similar to taking your vehicle to a service station for an oil change but telling the station you want to supply your own oil.

I finally found someone to do an updated appraisal without visiting the site. He agreed to provide us with an overview for a lot less money than a more comprehensive valuation would cost. At that point, the alarm bells should have been ringing, but if they were going off, I ignored the sound because I so wanted to believe the value of the equipment was what the old appraisal stated. I did my best to convince the bank to allow the simplest and quickest method of valuation, which turned out to be the equivalent of a drive-by real estate check.

If you drive by a house, it may look like all the others in the neighborhood, but once you get inside you realize the carpet is worn out, the sink is backed up, and the kitchen needs updating. There are a lot of problems you would miss by not going inside. Furthermore, if in one subdivision you had five different auctions ten years ago during a booming economy, those houses would have brought a good price even though they were auctioned. However, if you try to sell those same houses in the midst of an economic downturn, they likely would be much less. If you wouldn't use a ten-year-old appraisal to buy a house, why in the world would you use one to buy a company? You shouldn't, of course. But I did—and what a dire mistake it was. I ended up paying too much for Mid-South, and it took years to fully admit my terrible valuation error.

So how should the appraisal process work? An important part of a business appraisal is getting an itemized, up-to-date list of the equipment and who manufactured it. The appraisal investigates how similar equipment is selling. As with real estate comps, the appraiser uses comps from recent machinery auctions. In the case of an asset purchase, it's also crucial to know how useful the equipment is in today's environment and how well it has been maintained. I didn't consider depreciation issues, and as a result paid too much for the equipment in this respect, too. But most important: is the machinery in good working order? My speedy appraisal didn't even address this vital bit of knowledge. I didn't find out until after closing that many pieces of equipment were in need of repair and were not even running.

It almost makes me sick to think I was this foolish just because I was anxious to get the deal closed. My takeaway from this excruciating lesson is that if a buyer can't afford to do a current appraisal, he or she should at least get a third party that knows the equipment and business to provide some guidance as to the current value. If I had even taken this one relatively simple step, I'm quite sure I wouldn't have proceeded without a substantial reduction in price.

25

Short-cutting due diligence causes long-running headaches. Trimming money from your due-diligence budget can cost you dearly. Due diligence will reward you only if you really do it!

Clayton and I finally agreed on a seven-figure price for Mid-South, including some valuable raw material that mysteriously disappeared prior to closing. Its absence had a significant impact on the available cash flow, as we already had a scrap metal dealer lined up to buy the raw steel from us for sixty thousand dollars. Mid-South had purchased the steel for one of its jobs, and it had been sitting behind the plant for years. Since it wasn't needed for any of our production requirements, my plan was to add the cash from its sale to our working capital after the Mid-South deal closed. The bank lending officer had whittled our loan values down, down, and down some more each time negative news was uncovered prior to closing, so we desperately needed that money for working capital.

I didn't confront Clayton about its disappearance, and that was another terrible mistake on my part. I so valued his experience and expertise that I was afraid if I confronted him he might get angry and refuse to help with future engineering efforts or wouldn't refer us to the many potential customers that had tried for years to get Clayton to do work for them. Consequently, my silent partners and I were left to make the necessary repairs to buildings and equipment with cash that should have been reserved for payroll, utilities, and other necessities.

The missing raw material is a good example of how poorly I handled the entire situation. The disappearance not only created a shortfall in the cash I expected for operations, but it also created a trust issue for me with Clayton. I rationalized that it was easier just to forget about the missing material and focus on getting our business together started on a solid footing. Besides,

I didn't want to get into a battle over the cash when the only solution would have been for him to write a check for the raw material.

The missing steel was the first nail in our coffin, but I didn't have a clue about its devastating impact until almost a year later. I fooled myself into believing I had negotiated a good deal because of the extensive equipment I purchased, and the detailed pages describing each piece only made these feelings stronger. My unrealistically high confidence level lasted the whole time I was an owner of Mid-South and proved to be a serious detriment to my partners and me.

Patton Principle

26 **Hold everyone accountable, every time.** Trust issues don't magically go away if you let someone step outside the boundaries of integrity. It may be uncomfortable to confront a co-worker, partner, or other key business associate, but bringing to light a legitimate concern is worth a few ruffled feathers—and it just may save your business!

Under the terms of our purchase agreement, Clayton retained the land and buildings and rented them to our newly formed corporation under a long-term lease. He gave us first right of refusal to purchase the land and buildings in the event someone else wanted to buy them. Although Clayton would have preferred to sell us the land and buildings, we just couldn't get our bank to fund that additional debt. In fact, the bank continually applied pressure to reduce the amount of our loan, and in the end we borrowed much less than our original projections showed that we needed.

Purchasing the assets but not the land and buildings was another big mistake. For some businesses, it is not as important to own the actual real estate because the assets can readily be moved to another facility if necessary. In the case of a tool and die shop, however, some of the die equipment can be easily relocated, but for others, such as presses, moving them simply isn't feasible. Not only is such equipment bulky and heavy, but whatever portion of machinery is visible above ground, there is an equal amount beneath the surface, buried in a hole and covered in concrete. Trying to move a press to another facility is not like moving a desk or couch, and the cost to try is prohibitive.

Securing a multi-million dollar line of credit for Mid-South required financial projections including a balance sheet, profit and loss statement, and cash flow projections. Although I had some familiarity with the terms, I didn't fully understand the relationship between these financial tools. It's one thing to read about financial terms and quite another to apply that knowledge to a real-life situation. When the bank asked me to make a financial forecast, I realized how much I didn't know. Nevertheless, I did my best to comply.

My projections were based on starting a business from scratch, because with the exception of M & M, we had no other real customers at the time my partners and I took over Mid-South. In the process of pulling together information for the bank, I learned a lot about loan officers. It seems they almost always look for ways to trim anticipated costs and expenses. Bankers try to reduce the borrowing level depending on their level of confidence in the borrowing party's operating personnel.

The bank wants to reduce its exposure to risk, and many times a banker's "gut" tells him the borrower is asking for too much money. As a result, the banker will start asking questions targeted at the manufacturing operations where such price inflation might well take place. For instance, the payroll might include a few too many people, or some of the salaries may be too high. This is how an experienced banker can "hammer" a borrower's plans here and there, eventually reducing the loan amount by 25 percent or more.

The loan we requested was no different, and the officer assigned to us didn't want to loan us a single penny more than was absolutely necessary (you would think the opposite, given that the bank is in business to loan money and earn an interest rate in exchange). Getting the loan approved was exhausting and took weeks, not just days, and the amount we ended up with limited our spending for getting the plant back up and running. Much to our dismay, the original loan was reduced by 35 percent—yet another reason it was a terrible mistake for us to proceed with the project.

We should not have moved ahead with that bank but instead looked for another more familiar with the manufacturing industry. My problem was that I didn't want to let the lender go, out of fear I would not find another one for the Mid-South acquisition. Another consideration was that the time invested with this banker could not be duplicated easily, and the timeline with the seller fairly well prohibited starting over from scratch with a different lender.

Patton Principle

27

If you're doing something out of fear, stop doing it. Fear is a terrible reason to make a business decision. Few things are as bad as you think they might be unless you let fear take over. If you're tempted to move ahead because you're afraid not to, stop and make yourself look for other options.

I absolutely should have walked away from the bank—and even the deal—when the loan amount was reduced. But I was brimming with optimism over the great deal I thought I had negotiated, not realizing that my lunch was being eaten right in front of me.

Progress was slow right after the acquisition, but gradually, Mid-South's equipment once again came to life. A new paint job dramatically transformed the shop's appearance, and we added electronics to some pieces of equipment to increase the precision needed for closer tolerances that the current customer base demanded. Of course, these improvements also created additional drains on our available cash.

Initially, we had three short-term goals. The first was simply to get three pieces of equipment running together at the same time. Next, we sought to have three paying work-orders for customers all in process at the same time, and third, we wanted three transfer truckloads of completed work shipped to customers in a single twenty-four hour period.

During the final stages of retrofitting, while still handling my Rheem accounts, I began to call on new and old Mid-South customers such as Ford Motor Company, Thomas Industries, Briggs & Stratton, and Tennsco, to name just a few. Clayton also gave me a list with the names of one hundred former or prospective customers, and I was determined to speak with each one of them. I discovered, though, that many had been bought out or had gone out of business.

For those I could contact, I started by making an introductory phone call to the plant manager or chief engineer of any potential manufacturing customer. If that went well and we found common ground between our capabilities and their needs, I set up a face-to-face meeting. If that went well, I invited the prospect for a Mid-South plant tour, where I tried to impress by demonstrating that we could produce on a timely basis anything we happened to be quoting or targeting for future opportunities down the road.

After going through this process with potential customers, I often received detailed tooling prints and specifications to quote a job. If awarded a competitive bid, I became the watchdog to help supervise the work back at the shop. Many times the tooling, dies, or other related items needed to produce an order would be supplied by the customer. In completing the work, Clayton did prove to be the valuable resource and sounding board I expected, thanks to his extensive experience in manufacturing.

Although he had no formal education, he was a brilliant tool and die man. He often reviewed my job quotes and warned that they were too cheap. My challenge was that job-shop manufacturing was highly competitive, and if my bid was too high, we wouldn't get the business. Although I certainly didn't like coming in too low either, many Wednesdays arrived without my having money in the bank for Friday's payroll, so in my desperation for cash to keep operations going, I was willing to take on most any job.

Fortunately, Clayton was not my only highly valued human resource. With grayish work pants stained by hydraulic fluid on the knees, both sleeves of his faded gray work shirt rolled up to his elbows, and steel-toed work boots that never saw a coat of shoe polish, James looked like a press operator right out of the 1950s. A cigarette hung from his lips as if it had been there for days, and his yellowing teeth confirmed the long habit he had with the "smokes."

James was known as "Popper" because of an unusual speech impediment dating back to his childhood. He stuttered and made a popping sound whenever he opened his mouth to try to form a word. James said I could call him Popper like everyone else, but I never did. I thought it was a demeaning nickname, so I always called him by his real name.

James, his lazy youngest son, and a daughter-in-law who was long divorced from his eldest son were the only three workers in the press shop. They saw me as an invader of their private Mid-South domain and kept their distance from me. The turning point in my relationship with James came one day when, in a moment of despair, I walked into the press room, plopped down on the grungy couch, and dropped my head between my hands. The cumulative stress of problems in the office, unpaid bills, and die-shop drawings that needed final approval had all but crushed my spirit. There also were newly approved engineering drawings that needed raw materials, but I had no money to order them.

My only escape was the stamping shop. Little did I realize that the simple act of seeking refuge in James's press shop—a place few dared enter without his permission—would form an indestructible bond between us. James came over, patted me on the shoulder and, in his stammering way, asked what was wrong. Without looking up, I began pouring out my heart, telling him all the people and places that were demanding money I didn't have.

"I'm feeling such enormous pressure from it all, and I just wanted to come down here to find a little peace," I confessed.

James walked away quietly. A few moments later his daughter-in-law came over to me and said James asked her to tell me, "No one will hurt you here."

She went on to explain that James didn't like me when I first came to Mid-South, but that had changed since he'd seen me here regularly in the morning before he arrived and still here at night when he left. He'd also seen what I did to fix up the press shop—things Clayton would never do, including allowing them heat in the winter and a repaired plumbing line to the water fountain for just the press shop.

"He realizes you've put your heart and soul into getting this place fixed, and he wanted me to tell you that whatever you ask him to do, he'll do it."

From that day forward, James became a problem solver and trusted ally. As the months went by and we added new employees, I would always ask them to go visit James in the press shop as a final pre-employment requirement. As the prospect returned to my office, I would look out my office window across the open space between the office and press shop and finally through the door to the press area to see James. A nod from James and we would hire, but if James shook his head, I would pass on that particular prospect. To this day, I count James as the best human resources director I have ever had.

Before the day I confided in him in the press shop, James never came to the tool and die shop employee meetings. Afterward, he showed up regularly, along with his son and daughter-in-law. The third time they attended a meeting, I had a cake waiting for them that said, "Welcome press shop." We finally were unified like a family.

Patton Principle 28

Sharing your weakness with the right people at the right time can be a great strength. Sometimes your closest associates need to know you're human. While "keeping up the image" is necessary at times to be an effective leader, so is letting your inner circle participate in your struggles. You'll be surprised how motivating it is when they find out you truly need their help.

My workload was now more hours each day than when I attended Athens Vo-Tech during the day and built Big Ben Alarm Clocks on second shift. Back then, my day started at 7:30 a.m., and I finished my shift at West Clock at 11:30 p.m. Now, I worked harder but was much happier, because I was running my own company. I also agreed with Theresa to get another priority straight and started attending the Wednesday evening dinner and prayer time in the church where we were married. We also started attending Sunday school. Our newfound interest in church and God was tied directly to the stresses of running out of money at Mid-South.

My Rheem job (yes, I was still working there, too) provided me with great flexibility as I strained to bring Mid-South back to life. Then, without warning, I was forced to resign in good standing after nearly twelve years, and that caused a huge loss of personal income. I had long ago cashed in my 401(k) and invested it in Mid-South. And shortly after opening the doors for business, my other partners refused to invest additional capital since the short and long term outlook seemed hopeless.

Because Theresa and I had sold our home to invest the proceeds in Mid-South and because of the lack of cash available from the company, I suddenly had no way to feed my family and pay rent. Mid-South consumed every penny I gave it, and it needed much more than my original projections called for. To feed the voracious Mid-South beast, I borrowed from anywhere I could—from friends, relatives...and the IRS. Our cash flow problem got so bad that I stopped sending withholding taxes to the government. My other partners were done for sure at this point, and I was close.

New work was coming into Mid-South, but it became increasingly apparent that I was in over my head largely because I didn't fully understand the cash flow requirements of running the business. I was getting squeezed in all directions, and friends and partners (except one limited partner named Jim) had long since stopped returning my phone calls. My dream was quickly becoming a nightmare.

The original deal structure called for rent to kick in as revenues increased above a certain amount, which Clayton was all too happy to remind me about every time he walked the aisles.

"I see all this work, Jim. It's unbelievable what you've done here. But when are you going to pay me the rent you owe?" he asked.

I tried explaining that despite the activity, there was no money in the bank to pay rent. He persisted, and I knew the time had come to start paying him for the buildings, office space, and showroom. These were the same buildings in which my small team and I had invested time and money. We fixed gaping holes in the roof and painted the outside to look almost new for the plant tours that I conducted with prospective new customers. Likewise, we repaired, calibrated, rewired, painted, and got nearly every single piece of old equipment running just like in its prime. This was the same equipment disgruntled workers short-wired years ago when Clayton and his partner just turned out the lights and went to Florida to break the union's attempt to organize. The new digital instrumentation we installed made the place look almost like one of the high tech shops I had to compete against day in and day out.

I did not have enough money to pay rent and the weekly payroll, so I just paid our employees—which now numbered eighty—hoping Clayton would give me some additional time to come up with the rent. Instead, he seized on my weakened state of delinquency and reported it to the bank that held my loan.

I had personally guaranteed the loan, so the late payments now boomeranged back on me. The bank called the loan on my partners and me, which turned out to be the proverbial straw that broke the camel's back. The vendors, customers, and angry bank all proved to be too much for me.

The problem was actually made worse since one of my partners was employed in a highly visible position by the bank that held the loan. At that time, banks were under great scrutiny by the government for "brother-in-law loans," and although that was not the nature of our loan, there was pressure on the bank to take action. After a hastily called Mid-South stockholder's meeting, everyone agreed it was time to give up the fight and return the keys to Clayton, as agreed upon in the original agreement, to avoid a prolonged fight. I was devastated–and penniless.

I will never forget going home night after night, trying to be a good father and husband, when the pressure at work was killing me. My dear wife could see it all over my face. She provided wonderful meals, a clean home, and took good care of our young son, Spencer, during this extremely stressful period of our lives.

Weeks before the bitter end and for the first time since I was baptized, I prayed for help. I had exhausted all other options to save Mid-South, and nothing worked. At night, I laid awake with both hands covering my face, knowing I was about to lose everything.

Now, in desperation, I finally reached the point where I was willing to get down on my knees, with my face to the floor, and cry out to God. In my Mid-South office, with tears flowing, I cried out to Jesus to save my company. I knew He had done many miracles while on earth; perhaps He would do another one and bail me out of this mess.

"Please, dear Lord, don't let me lose everything! Please help me, dear God!"

Patton Principle

29

God won't let you have your way until you let Him have His. Life's greatest "success" comes from walking faithfully with your Creator. He wants you to put first things first—that means Him. Nothing else matters by comparison, and He will do whatever it takes to have a relationship with you.

My prayers were to no avail—at least from a human perspective—and the heartbreaking day came when I handed the keys back to Clayton. It was hard not to be bitter about this outcome, especially since when I bought the company from him, almost two years ago to the day, it had been in such terrible shape. Without spending a dime, Clayton got both plants fixed, most of the equipment running, a newly trained work force, and a strong customer base with a back-log of profitable business waiting in the wings.

He turned around and paid the bank loan off with some of the money he received from my partners and me when we first purchased Mid-South. After sweeping out my old office, which I felt God led me to do as a last measure of humility, I said good-bye to everyone in both plants and the office, got in my car and drove off, never to return.

That evening, I sat on a knoll overlooking the tennis courts at an upscale country club with a tennis friend. I was thirty-one, the bottom had dropped out of my life, and I saw no way to recover. Tears streamed down my face in the greatest stress and sense of defeat I had ever known.

I blurted out, "My life is over."

Turning Point

My zeal for the deal led me astray, but in the process, I found the real deal.

In my haste to reach my career destination, I ran past three important stop signs that I should have heeded, but enthusiasm and naïve optimism clouded my judgment. As a result, no matter how hard I tried to turn Mid-South around, I had to face the fact that I had entered the deal with what the Bible calls "zeal without knowledge." But I didn't leave Mid-South completely empty-handed. I had gained things of real value: experience and a commitment to turn my life over to God, no matter where He might lead me.

Turning on a Dime 8

A few days after losing Mid-South, I received a phone call from Mike, my partner from the tanning spa venture. Mike was a good friend, and we had been playing tennis together since I had moved to Nashville in December of 1979. About ten years older and the co-owner of a successful company, Mike was like a big brother to me and was someone I greatly respected. In many ways we were complete opposites. I'm outgoing and sales-oriented while he is quiet, reserved, and analytical. Because we played tennis nearly every week, Mike was aware of the difficulties I went through with Mid-South and knew I was facing the most difficult challenge of my life. I was two weeks away from living on the street with a wife and small child.

He called to schedule a tennis match, but Mike had more in mind than just our next game. After playing for an hour or so, we took a break, and Mike asked me how things were going. I recounted the financial disaster that had just occurred and the emotional trauma I was going through. He understood better than most people, because as a business owner he had experienced a number of ups and downs himself. When I finished, Mike said he had an idea he wanted to discuss with me.

"Jim, I've known you for twelve years now. I've seen you dabble in this business and that business. You've had your hand in a number of different places, but I'd never seen you apply yourself 100 percent to an effort until you acquired Mid-South. You hung in there when things got tough, and you kept putting everything you had into the company. That was very uncharacteristic of you, compared with what I had seen in the past."

"I didn't have any choice," I explained. "After leaving Rheem, Mid-South was my sole income. Once I started investing every penny I had in it, I literally could not do anything but stay with it."

"I understand that," he replied. "But it made an impression on me that you finally focused all your efforts on one thing. Now what are you going to do?"

"I don't know, but I desperately need a job."

"Where are you going to get the job?"

"I'm thinking of going to New York or Georgia or someplace and try to get a job similar to what I was doing at Rheem."

"Well, I have a proposal for you."

"You do?" I said with excitement I had not felt in much too long.

Mike was in the overhead power line construction business. His company installed telephone poles and strung the wires. Cities replace telephone poles regularly so there was an ongoing need for his company's services.

"Jim, I've been in business for twenty-one years, and this is the third down cycle I've experienced. The first one almost put me out of business. The second one I saw coming, so I was prepared for it and weathered the storm a lot better. Now, we're in the third one and I'm 100 percent ready for it. And I know we're going to come out of it," he said as my thoughts began racing, wondering what he had in mind.

"What I'd like to do is offer you an opportunity to find an acquisition that I could bolt on to my company."

Buying and integrating a company into an existing one is not an easy process because two companies usually conduct business in very different ways. Many people in the mergers and acquisition business claim the work on an acquisition just begins with the transfer of ownership. The heavy lifting starts when two distinct corporate cultures have to be integrated.

Mike not only asked me to find a suitable acquisition, but also to value the deal and manage the integration of the new company into his business. The reason he approached me, he explained, was because he saw how I grew Mid-South. He liked the way I interacted with the people there, and he was impressed with my ability to hang on no matter what.

"I'll give you ninety days to find a potential acquisition. But before I make the official offer: what is the most important thing you learned from this Mid-South experience?"

It was an excellent question, and I thought about it before responding.

"You know, Mike, I'll never pay too much for another business."

While I was excited about his offer, I also knew this was going to be a formidable challenge. Finding a suitable company outside Mike's normal territorial boundaries, one we could acquire within ninety days but without paying too much, would be like looking for a needle in a haystack. Nevertheless, I quickly accepted the offer. We settled on a salary, shook hands, and Monday morning I arrived at work in coat and tie.

Mike and I immediately began developing my game plan for the next ninety days. He made it clear from the beginning that he was not going to manage my time. Mike was only interested in the results, which would be very easy to determine at the end of ninety days. Either we had a new company or we didn't.

Initially, I searched for potential acquisition targets within the company's geographical footprint, which covered several southeastern states. His company was a member of a contractors' association, and the membership provided a good starting point for prospects. I also used the same SIC codes by which I found Mid-South.

I kept alert for prospective companies through word of mouth from the banking and finance sources used by industry contractors and auction companies. I researched bankruptcy filings, and finally, after doing my homework, I began making cold calls to see if anyone knew of a company the ownership might be interested in selling or that was in financial trouble and needing to find a solution in short order. I had no way of knowing that a corporate decision five hundred miles away would enable us to find a perfect bolt-on.

Charlotte, North Carolina-based Duke Power Company unexpectedly made a major change in one of its business models that affected the company's relationship with its many electrical contractors. Duke had been using a cost-plus method and overnight switched to a competitive bidding process. This new strategy meant that Duke would use only one large contractor to cover Duke's entire market area rather than using smaller contactors in limited geographical areas as it had done previously.

As a result, many small but well-established overhead power line companies were forced out of business. Suddenly, there was a large pool of potential employees available. The Duke Power change created rumblings within the industry and resulted in massive publicity.

When I heard the news, I keyed in on companies in the Carolinas, Georgia, and parts of Florida that were affected by Duke's decision to see if I could find one which met Mike's acquisitions criteria. I arranged face-to-face meetings with upper management and owners of many of these contractors. Y. C. Ballenger Company was one of the contractors, but it had already filed for bankruptcy. Headquartered in Greenville, South Carolina, Ballenger was a well-run, seventy year-old overhead power line construction business almost identical to Mike's company. The company had been highly successful working with Duke under the cost-plus arrangement, but now it was fighting for its life.

Mike and I scrutinized Ballenger as a potential acquisition because it met our criteria of a company with financial weakness and excessive overhead, equipment, and real estate. Ballenger's assets included several buildings for storing inventories and fenced areas to park the fleet of well-maintained trucks and trailers used for field service work.

Acquiring a business out of bankruptcy is an entirely different matter than acquiring a business through normal channels. There are intricate laws pertaining to corporate bankruptcy, and there are bankruptcy experts who specialize in working through the process. In many ways, I didn't know how much I didn't know, so I pursued Ballenger with the Lord's guidance and direction, and we ended up at the conference table at a time when everyone else had thrown in the towel and walked away.

There's a saying in the M&A world that you should always try to be the last one at the table with the seller, and that's what happened to us. We acquired Ballenger by simply making its payroll one week. The company had issued checks to employees but did not have sufficient funds in the bank to cover them. Mike provided the money for payroll, and we instantly took over a business which had more than three hundred employees prior to Duke's contractual change and still had an impressive list of motorized equipment and buildings.

Ballenger also maintained other profitable contracts and was pre-approved to submit bids on state and federal contracts. Any one of these assets was worth many times the amount of that one weekly payroll.

"Wow, Jim, you didn't pay too much for that one!" Mike was clearly satisfied.

Even though finding an acquisition had been my focus during those ninety days, there were still aftershocks from my Mid-South disaster. Late one Friday afternoon amid the Ballenger negotiations and due diligence, a phone call deflated any optimism I was enjoying. A lady, who identified herself as an agent of the Internal Revenue Service, was on the other end of the line with an ultimatum: either admit my debt for unpaid employee holdings from Mid-South and begin a repayment plan or face legal action. I agreed to cooperate and scheduled a face-to-face meeting with the agent.

At Mid-South, I had indeed withheld taxes from employees, but I didn't turn in the funds to the IRS because of my chronic lack of working capital. (Can you say, "Big mistake"—again?) Now, Theresa and I were personally liable for those funds!

A few days later, Theresa and I sat across the table from an IRS agent who was not at all what I expected. A kindly, pleasant lady, she looked and sounded like a grandmother. As I explained all that happened and how we lost our home and savings, she became sympathetic toward our plight and made every effort to work with us. Still, Theresa and I had to go line by line with her through our personal checkbook to review payments and deposits to validate that we in fact had more expenses than income from the previous months.

After a couple more meetings to hammer out an accounting for all previous taxes, we agreed on a compromise to settle our debt with the IRS. We scheduled a date to sign the Offer to Compromise agreement, and our agent said she would call us to confirm the arrangements. The day before the scheduled signing we still had not heard from her, so I called her office and heard news I could hardly believe: our IRS "grandmother" had died suddenly, and I would need to call back because my case was being reassigned to another agent.

In addition to my sadness over this woman's untimely death, I now had to start over with someone else at the IRS. I contacted the new agent in hopes of proceeding with the scheduled signing under the agreed-upon terms. After a brief introduction and explanation of the terms to which we had agreed, a stern voice on the other end replied, "I'm not going to give up that much; I can promise you that right now." The stern voice became demanding and informed me that the previous agreement was no longer valid.

By telling my story of how much money Theresa and I had already lost and explaining that we had borrowed money from family and friends to make it this far, I tried to get him to understand that we simply didn't have anything left to give. Nevertheless, the agent insisted we come up with another $10,000.

Providentially, Mike paid me a $10,000 net bonus in addition to my salary for successfully acquiring Y. C. Ballenger. So my happiness at completing the acquisition of Ballenger was tempered by my disappointment at having to fork over my entire bonus to the IRS. However, Theresa and I didn't renege on our promise to tithe 10 percent of our gross income. From the day I asked the Lord to save Mid-South, Theresa and I agreed we would tithe from whatever income we earned, regardless of whether we had sufficient funds to meet our obligations. Our reason for tithing was not because we thought that by doing so, God would reward us and make us wealthy. Rather, we did it because God commands His people to tithe, and we were simply being obedient.

30

Giving isn't important—it's essential. Although the blessing of giving always comes back to the giver, the best reason to give is because it's the right thing to do. Find worthy causes—your church, a mission, a non-profit organization that helps the poor—and make giving to them a top priority in your financial life.

While the Ballenger acquisition substantially increased Mike's corporate revenue, my share of the deal was limited to the agreed-upon compensation for the ninety-day period, plus the bonus money. It was a fair arrangement because Mike had taken a gamble with me, and he was handsomely rewarded. From that point forward, I became an equal partner with Mike. We formed PPMC, Inc.

Since Mike's company already had expertise in building power lines, the acquisition ran smoothly, but it was still a lot of work to integrate the companies. Terry, the president, and I joined forces to handle the numerous transitional and operational issues.

As with any acquisition, the takeover and integration was accomplished in phases. Each department had responsibilities to mesh the new with the old. For example, while we retained the payroll administrator at Ballenger, this employee had to be retrained in a new method of payroll.

The ongoing business is important, especially customer satisfaction. Very few employees had ever experienced a complete company takeover, but most of them had good attitudes. For those who didn't, it was management's job, as a last resort, to terminate them and hire new employees.

Once we signed the acquisition agreement, I started spending Monday through Thursday in Greenville to manage the merger. On weekends, I came home to be with my family. On my first day at Ballenger, I hit the ground running and set up a "war room" in the conference room. This became my office over the next several months as I assumed control of the transitional side while Terry took control of the field operations, which included the crews that worked in teams on specific jobs.

One of my first responsibilities was to outline the immediate tasks needing completion in order to keep the integration on track. I made a list which included the name of the person responsible for each task and displayed it on one of many paper boards hanging on the four walls of my war room.

I implemented a policy that any check in the amount of fifty dollars or more had to come through me for signing. At first I got quite a bit of push-back, as people told me it was ridiculous and impractical, given that there could be two hundred checks issued each day.

"Okay," I said, "Bring them in because I want to know about each one."

On some days, a stack of checks arrived three times for my review and approval.

We implemented a payment schedule so all of our suppliers, vendors, outside contracting services, and utilities became accustomed to how we paid our bills. I also set a goal of finding one cost-saving measure a day. It could be as simple as buying coffee in bulk rather than from five different sources. By consistently searching for and implementing new cost-cutting ideas, we gained substantial savings. In addition, we cut costs by combining office supply purchases when buying for both companies, and we secured joint company discounts with freight lines. We even looked at ways to save money on uniforms, packaging costs, and the like.

Having two businesses headquartered hundreds of miles apart caused some tension at first. The employees of Ballenger were both mourning the loss of what was familiar and adapting to changes. Eventually we smoothed things out and reminded everyone, regardless of where they worked, that they were now a part of a bigger, stronger company.

Every afternoon at 4:30 sharp, we held a management meeting in the war room. The wall charts were organized so each tear-off sheet had a heading such as Accounting, Accounts Payable, or Accounts Receivable. Under each heading was a list of tasks which would not be removed until the task was complete. If we checked off all but one item, we hung a new sheet, but that remaining task stayed until someone was pressured into taking care of the unresolved issue. (I've found that displaying sheets of activities in meetings is effective, because they focus people on their specific responsibilities. More importantly, the embarrassment of an open item continually just hanging there can be motivating for the department responsible.)

Patton Principle

31

When you take the bull by the horns, don't let go. There are times when it's up to you and no one else. If you're in charge of handling a crisis, you probably need to become a control freak—at least until the danger passes. Other people may not like it at first, but eventually they'll respect your commitment and enjoy sharing the success of a business rescued from disaster.

While I experienced a satisfying level of success in managing the integration of Ballenger, I still considered my lack of formal training an impediment and secretly feared being embarrassed by getting asked business questions I couldn't answer. To compensate, I read everything I could about business and economics.

Partly because of my insecurity, I used to think asking a question was a sign of ignorance, but as I've gained experience, I've learned that asking a question is one of the most effective management tools there is. Open-ended questions are particularly useful. I might say, for example, "I don't understand the cash flow here" and wait for a response. The answer might be very revealing. I know the responses I got from questions I raised about Ballenger's expenses and processes gave me great insight not only into why things worked the way they did, but also into what changes needed to be made.

Several months into our first merger, Mike brought me a small article from *The Wall Street Journal* about a publicly traded holding company in Florida named Southeastern Public Services. It was being forced to sell all its holdings, which consisted of seventy companies. New York-based Triarc, also a publicly traded company, was the purchaser.

In such an acquisition, it's normal for a holding company of Triarc's size to cherry-pick the most profitable businesses from a conglomerate and sell or close the other businesses. Mike knew that within this conglomerate there was a construction contractor for a power line business called Wright & Lopez, which he thought would be an ideal acquisition for us. Because Mike had been following Southeastern for many years, he knew the company background and thought we should try to buy Wright & Lopez.

The next day, I put a call into Triarc. After a brief introduction, I told the receptionist I'd heard that Triarc had acquired the conglomerate. "I'm interested in buying one of the businesses," I said, trying to sound as professional as possible.

She put me in touch with Eric Kogan in Triarc's Corporate Development Department. Corporate Development oversees a company's buying, selling, or integration of a business, and the people in that department are typically sophisticated, hard-charging, no-nonsense professionals. Eric fit the mold precisely. When I told him I wanted to buy Wright & Lopez, he put me in my place by giving me a short lesson on the etiquette of how to approach a company about such an idea.

"Why in the world would you call me about a matter like this?" he asked incredulously. "If you are that interested, address it in a letter, kind sir." Click.

No goodbye. No nice speaking with you. It was just "click," followed by a dial tone.

Eric and I eventually became good friends, but during that first conversation I realized I must have committed a huge faux pas and immediately began typing a letter to him. Thanks to Clyde Switzer's mentoring, I felt confident that my letter form and punctuation were correct. Much to my dismay, though, I received no response for months. I called a few times without success, leaving messages that I was still interested in Wright & Lopez should Triarc decide to sell it.

Then, one day out of the blue, I got a call from Eric.

"You know, Jim, I remember your first call, and I do appreciate your letter. My colleague, John Kolan, and I are going to be in Atlanta, and we would like to have a face-to-face meeting with you."

Thrilled beyond words, I made arrangements to meet them in a hotel lobby near the airport. At the appointed time, I flew from Greenville, South Carolina to Atlanta.

As we talked, it soon became apparent that Triarc's primary interest in the conglomerate was its RC Cola Bottling Company and Wendy's fast-food franchising and store locations, which were global in scope. I tried to sound as impressive as possible by saying we were already in the overhead power line construction business in multiple states and wanted to add to those holdings.

Our conversation seemed to be going well as I explained my interest in Wright & Lopez and why it appeared to be an attractive prospect for PPMC. Then they dropped a bombshell I wasn't expecting.

"Who is your investment banker on this?"

I barely knew what one was and certainly didn't have an investment banker to refer to.

Eric and John made it clear they would need to speak with my investment banker before any further conversations could take place. They knew I was amateurish in my approach and wanted to validate that I could get a deal of this nature completed within an acceptable time period.

If their conversation with my investment banker proved satisfactory, they said they would provide me with financial information on Wright & Lopez. That way, I could formulate an offer based upon factual information from the historical and interim financials as well as operational insights about the organizational structure and its plant, property, and equipment (PP&E). This was my first exposure to working with a company such as Triarc for an acquisition, and every step of the process was on-the-job training for me.

As our meeting ended, Eric reiterated, "Okay, Jim, I'm looking forward to speaking to your investment banker in the coming days."

My mind flashed back to a meeting I had a few months prior with a Smith Barney stockbroker named Randy Campbell. He was based in Nashville, and I had recently retained him to manage my personal investments. Smith Barney owned an investment group in Atlanta called The Robinson-Humphrey Company, and Randy, knowing my line of work, had offered to introduce me to one of his firm's investment bankers in Atlanta whenever I had the need.

I agreed to have "my banker" get in touch with Eric, we parted company, and I called Randy. Not long after, Randy and I drove to Atlanta to get acquainted with Charlie Ogburn, a seasoned investment banker. A graduate of Vanderbilt University Law School, Charlie had practiced law before getting involved in investment banking. He was cordial and receptive to the idea of working with PPMC in future acquisitions.

Much to my disappointment, however, Charlie was extremely difficult to reach after our initial meeting. I tried unsuccessfully for months to get him to return my calls. At one point, I found out that he had been promoted, and I feared he was too busy to spend time with a small fry like me (a tribute to his rising-star status, he eventually was named co-head of Robinson-Humphrey's entire investment banking operation). My challenge was to convince Charlie to be my investment banker and advisor to help find the purchase funds and operating capital for acquiring Wright & Lopez from Triarc. Out of desperation and with a quick prayer to make Charlie available, I tried once again to reach him on the phone.

To my amazement and relief, I heard, "Charlie Ogburn." After a brief exchange of pleasantries, I described my predicament with Triarc.

"Let me get this straight, Jim. They want you to prove you can finance the deal before they will show you financials?" Charlie asked with a twinge of irritation in his voice.

I said yes, that was correct. But before I could finish my sentence he interrupted with, "I cannot believe the arrogance of requiring you to prove your financial capability prior to showing you the financials. Let's get them on the phone right now and talk with them. I'll put the call on conference, and you introduce me."

Hardly able to believe my ears, I dialed Eric's number.

When he answered, I identified myself and said, "Eric, I have Charlie Ogburn with Robinson-Humphrey on the phone. Do you have a moment to talk?"

"Absolutely. Hold on a minute, and I'll get John."

Once they were both on the line, their first question was whether this was the Charlie Ogburn who worked on a previous Triarc acquisition. Charlie confirmed he was the same person, and I had instant credibility.

Charlie took over the conversation. "Jim says you told him prior to your releasing financial information, or for him to even be able to make an offer to Triarc, you are requiring a conversation with his investment banker. Is that correct?"

With his normal, calm demeanor Eric said, "As a matter of fact, that is correct."

Eric asked Charlie if he planned on helping me raise the money for this acquisition, "because it will be in the $20 million range."

Nothing could have prepared me for what happened next.

Without missing a beat, Charlie shot back, "We wouldn't breathe deep to raise $70 million for Jim Patton under the appropriate circumstances."

After a moment of dead silence, Eric said, "Jim, if you will give me your mailing address, I will Federal Express the financial package to you for delivery tomorrow morning. We would be honored to work with you and your investment banker on this deal."

After hanging up with Eric and John, Charlie said, "Once you receive the financials and have digested them, let's talk about what role Robinson-Humphrey can play in this acquisition."

I replied with five or six rapid-fire thank-you's. Charlie, with a chuckle by which he is known around the world, said, "Okay, okay, Jim, let's see what the numbers look like. Give me a call after you've had some time to digest them."

The next day the financials arrived as promised, and I immediately began pouring over them. It quickly became apparent that Wright & Lopez was a large and complicated company with nine operating locations, including its headquarters in a bad part of Atlanta. The company employed some six hundred workers and owned more than eight hundred vehicles. Wright & Lopez even maintained the fiber optic telecommunication lines above and below ground that ran through Atlanta's Hartsfield International Airport. This particular piece of business required notification of any ownership change because of national security interests.

As I sorted through the mass of detail about Wright & Lopez, I realized there were nine distinct areas of the company with separate contracts, so I created nine stacks on the floor. For each section, I would evaluate the operations on a stand-alone basis and then back into my offer for the entire company.

One thing I had learned in the last year was that most established companies have excessive personnel. I hoped to formulate a company that would be managed from the top down. This would necessitate strong capabilities in the parent company to reduce duplications at the individual locations.

As I reviewed the stacks of contracts and financial data by operation, I noticed one disheartening thing they had in common: not a single area was making money. I asked myself how Triarc could expect to get $24 million for a business that offered only negative cash flow—something I was all too familiar with from my Mid-South days.

This time it was my turn to be blunt with the Triarc guys. I called Eric and explained that I had studied the financials for Wright & Lopez.

"I don't know where you came up with $24 million for a company that's losing money," I told him.

He laughed and said they thought the inventory was worth $30 million, so they discounted the entire company to $24 million. That meant they had not assigned any value to the contracts at all, most of which were to expire in twelve- to twenty-four months.

"The business is over fifty years old, Jim!" Eric continued, as he tried to sell me on the fact that its second- and even third-generation employees made for an especially desirable workforce for the next round of contracts.

While I was a novice in negotiations of this nature, I've since learned that this deal was just like any other potential acquisition. It was a typical situation in which the prospective buyer doesn't know how the seller valued the individual asset groups.

Even with a publicly traded company such as Triarc, the disclosures were hard to grasp unless one had a clear picture of the underlying financials. A consolidated balance sheet for a conglomerate will have many companies bundled together—which gives potential buyers access to that information—but it remains extremely complex without the Finance Department providing additional detailed insights into each company.

Through my years of buying and selling manufacturing companies, I've come to understand the importance of developing a valuation strategy based either on the assets of the business minus the liabilities or on its free cash flow (otherwise known as EBITDA—earnings before interest, taxes, depreciation, and amortization). Whichever approach a buyer assumes, there must be a viable strategic connection to another similar business, or the acquisition must fulfill a clearly defined and easy-to-understand strategic financial goal. Either way, the prospective purchaser's reasoning and the strategic fit of the acquisition play a vital role as to whether the prospect is accepted as a serious buyer or just a waste of the seller's time. (See Appendix 1, "KPAC Solutions' Approach to Valuation," which provides a more detailed explanation of this acquisition approach, including important insights into what constitutes a well-defined valuation of an ongoing business.)

As with any savvy seller, Eric's comments were intended to put Wright & Lopez in the best possible light. Even though it was losing money, he tried to convince me that the company's inherent value due to its long history and solid workforce were good reasons why it was worth $24 million.

Typically, a company like Triarc would have run a preliminary liquidation analysis to figure a worst-case valuation scenario for Wright & Lopez. The company had many assets literally on wheels (heavy duty trucks and specialized trailers) scattered throughout the southern United States. If all contracts were immediately terminated, Wright & Lopez owned a salable rolling stock of heavy equipment and expensive tools.

The traditional assets and liabilities were another important component of the Wright & Lopez value. The company's real estate holdings included numerous buildings and paved lots with fencing. In addition, there were accounts payable and various accrued liabilities complicating the overall valuation. Someone with industry-specific knowledge would have to invest considerable time to formulate a viable liquidation analysis, but Triarc had neither the industry knowledge nor the time to conduct such a study.

My own liquidation analysis came up with a valuation of only $7 million—less than 30 percent of Triarc's. The divergence in our numbers came about because I did not believe the assets would sell for as much as the balance sheet reflected, nor did I agree with Triarc's assumptions about the Wright & Lopez liquidation value. I knew that when one closes a business, revenue stops almost instantly, but the trailing expenses keep going and going as the selling of the remaining assets drags on. It can become a quagmire, and unless one is an experienced liquidator, it is easy to get burned in a situation like that. I recognized Triarc, not in the liquidation business, was used to owning only well-run businesses. That put me at an advantage in this situation.

I concluded that Triarc's expectations were overly optimistic, and because I did not have much experience liquidating a company either, I would err on the side of caution. In the worst case, I thought Eric's department would give a counter offer that we would kick around until settling on a price.

A simple example may help illustrate the art of setting a realistic value for a company. If a wholesaler of men's clothing goes out of business, the company will sell everything for a set price— an all-or-nothing deal. Let's say you are interested in buying the wholesaler's business, and you run your own analysis to establish a value for the inventory. Then you make an offer. The seller may tell you a retail value for the inventory, but will you really be able to sell the goods for that price? And what will it take for you to get them into the hands of buyers?

Some items may be hard to sell because they are unusual sizes or colors, while there may be other high-demand items which can be sold quickly and profitably. A portion of the inventory may be damaged—what's it worth in that condition? Another consideration is transportation costs. The seller wants you to pick up the goods and store them, and eventually you will need to ship the goods to buyers. What will that cost?

Unless you have sufficient cash on hand, you will need to get financing for the deal and figure in interest payments to the bank. You must determine what the inventory is worth to you, given your expenses, investment of time, and a realistic expectation of what you'll make on the deal. These and other factors need to be taken into account.

Also keep in mind that a forced liquidation is not nearly as attractive as an orderly one. With an orderly liquidation, the buyer has adequate time to examine and value the assets, do clean-up work as needed, advertise, and hire a professional auctioneer. In a forced liquidation, the process moves much more quickly, and the seller generally has only thirty to forty-five days to complete the process. As a result, goods typically are sold at fire-sale prices. "Strategic buyers" tend to pay a higher price because of their familiarity with the product and current consumer demand, but in some forced sales, there isn't adequate time to get the word out to them. Finally, the time of year of a forced sale can have significant implications for what the seller will net.

In valuing Wright & Lopez, it worked in my favor that Triarc wanted to deal only with credible people who could complete large transactions. From Triarc's perspective, Wright & Lopez was an ugly, odd-sized piece of inventory it didn't want but had to take as part of the all-or-nothing deal from Southeastern Public Service.

Because of my experience with the Ballenger acquisition, I understood Wright & Lopez's business and had an idea of what it would take to make it profitable. Eric and John faced multiple challenges. Besides not knowing the industry, they needed to unload a business whose contracts were worthless and to liquidate assets scattered over a nine-state territory. Trying to get all assets in one place to sell them would be overwhelming and time consuming.

Not only that, Eric and John had sixty-nine other companies to handle within the conglomerate they had just bought. Wright & Lopez was little more than a pesky mosquito I suspected they would love to get off their books. I reasoned if Triarc received an offer for the entire company which provided a swift exit, it might sell Wright & Lopez cheaper than if a potential buyer wanted to cherry-pick some assets and leave Triarc with stragglers that would take even more of their time to sell.

The nine Wright & Lopez contracts were with local Bell phone companies. The big unknown to me was whether I could save any of these contracts and continue operating. In the best possible scenario, I would save them all. In the worse case, I wouldn't save any and would have to liquidate the equipment in each market. I guessed that the most likely outcome was some combination of renewed contracts and others that would require liquidation. But I had no way of knowing how things were going to settle out.

Patton Principle

32 **The right people will keep things from going wrong.** Whether you're hiring an employee or choosing an outside professional for your team, searching until you find the right person is worth the trouble. Once that crucial "human resource" is in place, work starts to take care of itself.

Emboldened by my new-found credibility through Charlie Ogburn and my growing realization that Triarc had a mess on its hands with Wright & Lopez, I told Eric the company was a piece of junk. Instead of hanging up on me, he asked if I would formulate a proposal for him and John to review. I agreed, knowing I could discount the company assets much lower than their true net worth since Triarc lacked the expertise Mike and I had with either option—running Wright & Lopez or liquidating it.

The essence of my proposal was that I would try to save whatever contracts I could. For those that could not be saved, I would liquidate the assets and get 25 percent of the gross proceeds. Triarc would get 75 percent of the net proceeds. If I was successful at saving the contracts, I would pay Triarc two-and-a-half times the net-book value of the balance sheet after restructuring or in two years, whichever came first. I calculated that under the worst-case scenario, Mike and I would each make $1.5 million.

I had never put together a proposal of this nature and didn't know where to begin. I recalled a bookstore in town that specialized in technical and professional subjects, and there I found a book that addressed legal matters relevant for every business owner. Thumbing through the book, I was amazed—and more than a little pleased—to find a standard proposal for an acquisition. I used it as a guide for my proposal to Triarc, imitating what was in the book down to the last detail.

"Jim, this is one of the better proposals I've seen," Eric told me after receiving it. If he only knew, I thought to myself.

A few days later Eric called to invite me to New York to discuss the proposal in person. "We understand your concept but surely you are missing some asset valuations with your offer as low as it is," he said.

This was music to my ears because I knew I had room to go up if needed. The fact that they wanted the meeting was proof to me that we were not very far apart on valuation. Eric grumbled about not being my "bank," but I simply dodged that bullet by saying, "There is no bank on the face of the earth that would finance this mess." I could envision Eric smiling as if being caught with his hand in the cookie jar.

We arranged a meeting for the next day. Eric and John were busy people, and Wright & Lopez was a small player I knew they'd like to get out of their hair.

"Look, this sucker is not worth anything," I told them as we got down to business. "The best I could do is come up with a plan that would reduce the size of this business to something profitable; as I reduce it, I will be selling off assets," I said as we plowed through the proposal.

As operators in this industry, I explained that Mike and I could either put these assets back to work or liquidate them in a much more professional and expedited fashion than Triarc. I also offered post-closing transparency so that Triarc could see exactly what values were obtained either through the sale of assets or renewed contracts.

When I finished my pitch, Eric and John excused themselves and left the room. I fully expected them to come back and tell me to jump off a cliff, because anyone who studied my proposal carefully could see that I was in a no-lose position.

When they returned, John said, "We've thought about this, Jim, and we'd like to move forward."

I could hardly believe it. They didn't even counter my offer! I replied that to proceed with the deal, I would need a ninety-day standstill so they wouldn't discuss Wright & Lopez with anyone else. That would give me a fair chance to complete my purchase arrangements, and it would eliminate any potential that Triarc could exit with a third party.

"All right, we've got a deal," John said.

When I left their office, I looked back at the World Trade Center buildings along the skyline and took a deep breath, relishing the moment and the remarkable fact that my first trip to New York City had been so productive.

I flew home to Nashville the next morning and took Theresa to lunch. I told her our lives were getting ready to change, and change in a dramatic way.

"We're going to obtain a level of wealth you're going to find amazing."

Turning Point

Just when I thought my life was at a dead end, along came Mike with a plan for my personal turnaround.

And thank God for him. He was truly the friend who sticks closer than a brother as the Book of Proverbs references. When I lost Mid-South, I was broke and desperate. I owed more money than I could ever imagine repaying and truly believed I could never recover. I thought I had put my family in permanent financial bondage, and I saw no way out. It was God's mercy that sent Mike to me with his offer of employment, which helped me to see that God did indeed have plans for me—far better plans than I could have worked up on my own. I learned that no matter what the circumstances or challenges, His power can handle it. Nothing is hopeless for God. If we allow Him, He can use us to achieve things beyond our imagination. As my Christian walk grew, so did my understanding that, if I get out of the way, the Lord can take me places I never would have dreamed.

Turning Around
Fortune 1000-Owned Companies

"**I**f you terminate your contract with BellSouth, we will follow you wherever you go and to any other career you pursue. You can count on BellSouth being there to ruin you!"

Maybe this is going to be more difficult than I thought.

Up until Wright & Lopez President Rick Boyle and I walked into the BellSouth Operations Office in Birmingham, Alabama that Monday morning, no one had ever terminated a contract with one of the Ma Bells.

The general manager of BellSouth's Birmingham operations was dead serious. Not only did he mean to carry out his threat to me, but I knew he had the title and the muscle to back it up. Maybe I was in over my head. After all, who was I to be the first service provider ever to quit on a BellSouth contract?

Every BellSouth manager in the room offered his or her own version of an unfriendly smirk, while Rick and I slowly went pale. The GM was adamant he was not about to allow our company to leave BellSouth in the lurch.

At the time, neither Rick nor I fully understood what kind of disaster our withdrawal would cause BellSouth, but we were about to find out. He and I planned to meet with BellSouth executives in all the markets where Wright & Lopez had contracts with the telecommunications company. Birmingham, our first stop, was a major regional operations center for BellSouth in the early nineties.

The corporation Mike and I formed completed the acquisition of Wright & Lopez on a Friday, and the following Monday Rick and I were on center stage in the Birmingham conference room. More than a dozen executives were waiting for us when we walked in. Rick knew most of them, so the only introductions were of the top regional BellSouth officers and me as we sat around a large conference table. The meeting was formal, with no friendly smiles from either side.

As all eyes turned to me, I showed the BellSouth executives the exit clause in our contract and told them in eighty-nine days we would pull out more than150 employees, all their related equipment, and our around-the-clock support, which currently was available 365 days a year. You could hear a pin drop (even though it wasn't a Sprint meeting). In a whisper that became vicious as his volume increased, the BellSouth GM made his spiteful threat to ruin me if I attempted to withdraw.

"Let me be clear," I replied. "We will be gone in ninety days, because we're not making money here."

Rick and I had arranged this meeting under the auspices of introducing me as one of the two new owners, but my real purpose was to point out the explicit language in our contract that allowed us to give ninety days notice if we wanted to terminate the relationship. Prior to purchasing Wright & Lopez, I learned that BellSouth's corporate and regional offices knew Wright & Lopez was losing a great deal of money every month because of the new contract, which had been signed a year prior to my involvement.

Pleas from Wright & Lopez to BellSouth for relief from the ridiculously low prices in the contract—which should never have been submitted—fell on deaf ears. While Wright & Lopez won these contracts through competitive bidding, everyone at BellSouth knew the company was dripping in red ink, but Wright & Lopez appeared to be trapped.

As far as BellSouth was concerned, there was no way out. Like it or not, Wright & Lopez had to perform for the next three years of the contract. BellSouth was such a large customer that to do otherwise would have been suicide for Wright & Lopez, and the telecommunications management knew it. In fact, they seemed all too happy about it.

From the standpoint of our original acquisition strategy, the ninety-day deadline to cut losses was an absolute necessity. Rick's management team immediately made appointments with each BellSouth customer. Although Wright & Lopez had contracts in multiple cities in nine states, each held the same basic agreement as the one in Birmingham. BellSouth was by far our largest customer, and with those contracts we simply had to stop the bleeding. If we didn't, from the ninety-first day going forward, each day of losses would be coming out of Mike's and my pockets.

The other BellSouth operations with which we had contracts were instructed to let the Birmingham office handle termination issues related to Wright & Lopez, but we continued visiting the other regional BellSouth offices, delivering the identical message. Although every one of them thought I was bluffing, I assured them they were dead wrong and shouldn't underestimate our commitment to exercise the option to withdraw. Yet no matter how strongly we stated our intentions, nothing seemed to faze them.

Early in the process of acquiring Wright & Lopez, I believed I could make $2 million. There were many variables—among them getting BellSouth to agree to a price increase—but in the worst-case scenario, if everything fell apart with the customer and employee base, I calculated that liquidation would net at least $1.5 million. I had checked my math too many times to be wrong, which is what gave me the confidence to hold firm in my chess match with BellSouth.

Patton Principle

33

Have a good fall-back position so falling back won't hurt. Make plans to win no matter what. When your worst-case scenario still paints a profitable picture, you can move ahead confidently regardless of the "downside."

Payroll for Wright & Lopez's 300 employees was almost $500,000 every two weeks. The first week under Mike's and my ownership, we discovered we were liable for an additional payroll period we had not anticipated. Fortunately, I was able to get Triarc to cover the payroll funds, amazed at God's continued blessings and provision. Our deal was structured so that Triarc would provide the first ninety days of working capital since we all recognized the losses could not be stopped immediately. Like a large cruise ship, it takes time to turn to the left or right.

After the acquisition transaction was complete, Eric marveled and told me, "This is the first deal I've witnessed where we sold a business and instead of getting a check, we wrote a check."

I anticipated that most, if not all, of the Wright & Lopez contracts would not be renewed, so from day one, I began shrinking the company by selling off warehoused equipment and terminating employees who didn't have work assignments lasting more than two weeks out.

About thirty days after our meeting in Birmingham, we received a call from BellSouth's vice president of operations, inquiring about our manpower allocation plans for the next six months for the Birmingham area. Rick happened to be in my office when the call came through, and he took the call there. I stood nearby while Rick whispered mini-updates as the conversation progressed. Rick informed the man that we had less than sixty days left on our contract, and all our people and equipment would be leaving Birmingham exactly as I had explained to the management team a month ago.

I scribbled a note to Rick telling him to ask, "Didn't you guys take Patton seriously when he gave written notice of termination?" The response was a short "No," and the call ended a few seconds later. Rick and I really couldn't believe our ears as we continued the laborious process of extracting Wright & Lopez from Birmingham.

BellSouth continued to call as the deadline grew closer. During one conversation, Rick learned that BellSouth did not have other contractors in place to take over our work. The other locations faced a similar deadline.

Eighty days into the notice, Rick received a call that floored him—BellSouth wanted to meet with us again in Birmingham to discuss re-negotiations for all Bell-related contracts with Wright & Lopez. A week later, Rick and I sat in the same large conference room where we met eighty-seven days earlier. This time, the group was much smaller, with just a handful of decision-makers in attendance.

Rick had his computer open and plugged into the company's network to give him Internet access. He busied himself, pretending not to be nervous, but in truth, we were both on edge. As the meeting started, their concerns about Wright & Lopez walking off the job became obvious. My nerves calmed down immediately as I realized Rick and I had the upper hand in a big way.

In preparation for this meeting, Rick and I had reviewed the current pricing on more than fifteen hundred line items. This itemized structure allowed BellSouth to have us perform tasks with both sides having a predetermined price in place. The problem with the pricing, though, was that Wright & Lopez simply couldn't do the work that cheaply and stay in business. While the contract was a bad business decision by the former owners, Mike and I were not going to get stuck with it and lose our shirts. Our management team calculated we needed a 40 percent increase across the board for Wright & Lopez to retain all its employees and become profitable.

I wasn't listening as the BellSouth GM began with conciliatory remarks about the improvement he had seen recently in our responsiveness and quality of work. Instead, I was mentally rehearsing the speech I was about to give. We were losing $300,000 a month in Birmingham, which soured me to the point where just being in the city made me ill.

When the general manager finished, I began. "I would like everyone in this room to know I don't drive through Birmingham anymore. In fact, I only fly over it, and I still get nauseated at 35,000 feet."

As the room grew deathly quiet, I realized I had their undivided attention and for the first time in my life, I felt what real authority meant in the business world.

"Please listen and listen well," I said, looking directly at the man who previously threatened to follow me from this industry to the next if I withdrew from the BellSouth contract prior to its completion.

"Wright & Lopez is withdrawing from Birmingham in less than seventy-two hours. We have already given notice to have the water and electricity turned off in our offices in three days. Why on earth wouldn't you believe I would do it?"

"We don't want you to leave," one of the executives interrupted. "We obviously underestimated your resolve."

"We anticipated you might say that because who else is going to do this work for you?" Rick and I were holding aces in a poker game with BellSouth's senior management.

"Let me stop right now and ask you a question, because this has been bothering me ever since I bought the company and saw all these losses." I turned to the GM. "Were you involved in the selection of the contractors to do this work?"

"Yes."

"At the time did you realize the other contractors' bids were much higher?"

"Yes."

"So you knew Wright & Lopez was going to get killed on this deal."

"Yes," he said with a sarcastic chuckle, "I knew it."

I wanted to wipe that mocking smirk off his face with a left hook, and in my anger I made a snap decision that would have dramatic, unintended consequences.

"We have here for you the revised proposal put together after many days of careful analysis, but it is not complete," I said, with as much cool as I could muster. "You need to take these prices and double them across the board."

The response was swift and in rapid-fire succession.

"You have got to be kidding. That is ridiculous and extremely insulting!"

"You're out of your mind!"

"That's totally irresponsible!"

"How in the world could you ever think that would work?"

Despite the barrage, I was not the least bit fazed.

"It will take a 100 percent increase to make enough to stay," I said with the confidence of someone who has nothing to lose.

Rick couldn't hide the shock on his face at my boldness. "What are you doing?" he mouthed to me across the table.

The BellSouth executives asked to excuse themselves, with copies of our revised proposal in hand. About thirty minutes later, they returned to the conference room.

"We realize there has been some bad blood between us," the GM acknowledged. "Normally under these circumstances we would require a rebid, but we know you're not going to stay in business for ninety days without an increase. Under the circumstances, we would like to end things right here. We will give you a 100 percent increase."

After acting like we were out of our minds to expect it, BellSouth's Birmingham office had agreed to a new three-year contract with a 100 percent increase for every line item. In that one moment, we went from losing $300,000 a month in Birmingham to making a quarter of a million a month.

Instead of earning $1.5 million to liquidate Wright & Lopez's assets, I suddenly had to shift gears and make plans to run the company for at least three years under a new pricing structure in which I could potentially make $8 million!

Rick excused himself, went down the hall to use a phone, and called Wright & Lopez's Birmingham office. "Don't fire anyone," he said excitedly. "We're getting ready to rock and roll."

As the last BellSouth employee exited the elevator and the doors closed, Rick let out the loudest "Yahoo!" I'd ever heard him utter. Neither of us could believe what had just happened, and we excitedly recalled the details as we made our way to the parking level. As the BellSouth building grew smaller in the rearview mirror, Rick and I began to lay out a plan for reviving Wright & Lopez.

Patton Principle 34

When you're well armed, stick to your guns. A good negotiator knows when to compromise, but if you don't have to, then don't. There's nothing wrong with winning big now and then.

We had similar success with most of the other BellSouth contracts, although they had not been nearly as big a cash drain as Birmingham. For some of them, we needed only a 20 or 25 percent increase to be profitable, and of the nine BellSouth contracts, only two did not renew. Almost overnight, Wright & Lopez's BellSouth contracts had gone from losing buckets of money to becoming a fountain of cash.

After downsizing the company by a quarter of its original size, I now had to reverse course, rehire people, and begin growing Wright & Lopez to fulfill these contracts. My success, though, had created one gigantic problem: As you'll recall from my story of setting up the Triarc deal, I included an incentive in which I would pay two-and-a-half times the retained earnings book value at the end of two years on any contracts I saved.

In my proposal, I had made it clear that I didn't know what was going to happen when I attempted to renegotiate the Wright & Lopez contracts, but I assured Triarc that one way or another, things were going to change because the contracts were all losers. I explained that I planned to liquidate equipment and shrink the business as I terminated contracts that were not renewed to a profitable level. I also planned to sell off real estate as there was no need for offices and land if we lost contracts in those markets. In a year's time, I had explained, I could make a much clearer decision as to whether it was better to stay in business or liquidate everything. If it turned out to be worthwhile to keep the company, I would pay Triarc two-and-a-half times the book value. Otherwise, Triarc would get 75 percent of everything sold.

I believed the most likely scenario was that I would liquidate everything and, after paying Triarc and Mike, put $1.5 million in my pocket. Since I had convinced myself we wouldn't be able to save the contracts, I was confident in my two-and-a-half times offer. But it was an unwise and unnecessary incentive to include. After all, Wright & Lopez was losing $8.5 million a year, and never in my wildest dreams did I think I'd have to make good on it. I saw it, rather, as a clever way to offer something that was about as likely to take place as winning the lottery twice in a row.

When in my anger I told the Birmingham BellSouth executives they would have to pay a 100 percent increase from our proposal, which already had a profit margin built in, I wasn't factoring in what we would eventually have to pay Triarc. A victim of my own success, I found myself in a precarious position as a result of my aggressive negotiating. Not only would I have to pay all the profits to Triarc, but because of the multiple, I was in the ridiculous situation of having to liquidate the company in two years to pay all I owed. Even my $1.5 million was at risk! I had fixed Wright & Lopez and suddenly made it so profitable I couldn't afford to own it.

I saw that I was going to be in deep trouble, so about six months into the Wright & Lopez acquisition I asked for a meeting with Triarc. As promised, I had been sending monthly updates to Eric, and he and the other Triarc executives couldn't believe the openness and transparency I provided. To date, I had paid Triarc $4.5 million for liquidated assets. There were times in which I could have easily cheated Triarc without anyone being the wiser, but I never did.

Nelson Peltz, the epitome of a dealmaker and co-founder of Triarc, was aware of my upcoming visit. Nelson became one of the country's wealthiest men, with a net worth estimated by Forbes magazine at more than a billion dollars. He bought distressed companies, turned them around, and sold them for a handsome profit. Snapple, which Triarc reportedly purchased from Quaker Oats for $300 million and sold three years later to Cadbury Schweppes for $1.5 billion, was one of his greatest and most highly publicized success stories, but there were others as well.

Nelson and I had not met prior to this visit, except for a brief introduction when he stuck his head in the door as we were finalizing the last few details of purchasing Wright & Lopez, but he knew of me and my work. At one point, when Nelson had asked Eric about my trustworthiness, Eric assured me that he told Nelson, "I trust him 100 percent."

During my meeting, I explained that since acquiring Wright & Lopez from Triarc, I had shrunk the company as planned. To date, I had received $7 million of accounts receivable, $2 million from equipment sold, significantly reduced Triarc's liability for millions of dollars in performance bonds, and sold operations-related real estate.

"When I bought Wright & Lopez six months ago it wasn't worth anything," I said. "I still don't know how it will all work out, but I think I'll still be able to keep the company. After getting a handle on this business, I can get Triarc out of bonding liabilities for the rest of the performance bonds and buy you out now rather than waiting another year and a half to pay you."

"Okay, Jim, please review this deal with me at a little slower pace, if you don't mind," Nelson said as he turned toward me. "You and I both know that you put the tail-end kicker as an enticement for us to go with you so that if everything went exactly right, we would both hit a good (baseball) ground-roll double."

Nelson was now pacing back and forth along a high-rise window overlooking Park Avenue in the heart of business in New York City. "And now you're up here, and you want to pay me back early. You didn't have the money to do this deal with cash, and now you say you want to pay us in cash. Either you made a lot of money or something has come up that is going to make you a lot of money and you would rather pay us now than later. I'm inclined to turn you down because if I accept, I think I'm leaving some money on the table."

My heart sank. I was facing the king of dealmakers and had nothing with which to bargain.

"You have done a lot according to Eric," Nelson said, as he shifted his attention to him. "This guy has represented himself with integrity?"

"Absolutely," Eric replied.

"Out of all the companies we had, we thought Wright & Lopez would be the last company we would sell, and it turned out to be the first," Nelson continued. "What are you offering?"

"Two million," I answered weakly, hoping my voice wouldn't crack.

"Okay, we'll take it. You're going to make some money on this, and you deserve it." Nelson studied me, one huge deal guy eying a beginner whose poker hand had just been figured out.

Once again, I simply could not believe my ears. Relieved does not even begin to describe my emotions, and I remember silently thanking God for saving everything I had worked for and just started to achieve.

"Okay," I said as casually as possible. "Give me a little time to get the money together."

"Gosh, you don't have the cash?" Nelson was incredulous. "Then pay me in sixty days."

As Eric walked me out to the door, he looked at me with a smile that showed he gladly approved of what just had happened and said, "Man, he just threw you a bone."

And he had. Nelson could have held my feet to the fire to the point where I couldn't have afforded to keep the business and perhaps would have had to borrow money from Triarc to continue—all because of how well the BellSouth negotiations went. At the time I got the concessions from BellSouth, people thought I was an absolute genius at negotiating. I received lots of positive and admiring feedback, to the point where I became a little cocky because I knew I had gotten a good deal. However, the Lord has a way of humbling us, and before long I saw that I had outsmarted myself. My meeting with Eric and Nelson was yet another time when the Lord rescued me from what could have been disaster and served as a pointed reminder of Who is really in control.

As I look back on the experience, I regret not speaking the whole truth, even though doing so may have been very costly. Nelson had figured out there was good news somewhere—why else would I offer to pay early?—but he didn't press the matter and instead chose to take the $2 million I offered.

By not mentioning the new contracts with BellSouth, I was operating out of fear rather than faith. And faith that only works when there's nothing to lose isn't the true biblical faith Jesus calls us to live. I had performed morally and ethically in all other regards from the very beginning of my relationship with Triarc up to that point. Now this one issue caused me to stumble and compromise my integrity, something a Christian should never do.

Patton Principle 35 **Honesty is the best policy— regardless of the outcome.** You don't always have to wait for "the next life" to get a handsome pay-off for doing business with integrity. Other people can be the source of great blessing when they know you've played the game fairly. But without full disclosure, any pat on the back you may receive will be tarnished by the error of not providing the whole story and compromising your integrity.

Sixty days later, we paid Triarc in full and took sole ownership of Wright & Lopez. And several months afterwards, Mike left our partnership for personal reasons. I bought out his share, and PPMC became Patton Management Corporation (PMC).

Some time later Mike's company, filed for bankruptcy. It had gotten involved in some commercial jobs that went south, and

he simply could not recover. I learned about this sad development from Don Eden, whose brother's son, Terry, was president.
Mike also owned Eusco, where Don served as president. Eusco's
business involved mounting platforms to the back of heavy duty
utility trucks, to handle everything necessary to install telephone poles in the ground, as well as "cherry pickers" that lift
a lineman so he can work on electrical wires. Mike's power line
construction company was one of Eusco's best customers.

Don is a competent business operator and a person of high
integrity. Under his leadership, Eusco had been profitable from
day one. With Mike's other company going out of business, however, and the inevitable affect that would have on Eusco because
of joint ownership positions between Don and Mike, Don saw
the writing on the wall and resigned.

About a month later, Don called to let me know he had taken
a job as president of Telelect East, which did the same type of
work as Eusco but was much larger. It had assembly facilities and
administrative offices in Richmond, Virginia, and in Emmaus,
Pennsylvania, with hundreds of employees between the two
locations. I didn't know it at the time, but Telelect was owned by
a publicly traded company called Terex (NYSE: TXI).

"That's wonderful news, Don," I said, sincerely pleased that
he had landed such a good job so quickly—although it wasn't
really surprising due to Don's industry knowledge and operational expertise.

Two weeks after hearing about his appointment as Telelect's
president, I was surprised by another call from him.

"How are you doing, Don?"

"They fired me." He said with a level of emotion I didn't know
Don had ever expressed in his life.

"You've got to be kidding me. You were the president. Who
fired you?"

"A guy named Fil Filipov."

"Who is he?"

"He is the restructuring guy for Terex, the new owner of Telelect East."

"What's Terex?"

"Terex is a major heavy equipment manufacturer that's publicly traded on the New York Stock Exchange," Don said. "They acquired the Telelect East business."

"Well, Don, who is going to run the company?"

"Terex has a controller named Kevin Kennedy who was reporting to me, and I guess he is going to run it." He went on to explain that Kevin is a solid financial manager.

While we talked, Don piqued my interest when he said that Telelect East was part of a group of businesses Terex bought as a package. As with Wright & Lopez and Triarc, Telelect East was outside of Terex's core business.

"I can tell you right now that Terex does not want to be in a final-state assembly business like Telelect East. Terex only wants to manufacture the platform," Don said with confidence that I readily believed.

"If they don't want it, why don't we buy it?"

"Jim, Telelect East goes from Maine to Florida." Don's voice was now at the low end of the emotional scale, and knowing Don, this was very troubling to him because he always had control of his emotions (the direct opposite of me, regrettably).

"Well, you ran Eusco. You can run it," I said, trying to sound encouraging. "I've been working on a strategy of providing sellers with a comprehensive solution. If we go to Terex and say we will buy all of Telelect East, from Maine to Florida, they'll only have to deal with one buyer."

Don acknowledged that Terex had already been contacted by people who wanted to buy Telelect East piecemeal.

"We can come to the table, say that we will take the whole thing, and restructure the company after we purchase it once it is under our watch and ownership. Do you know who to talk to about buying Telelect East?" I asked.

"Yes, his name is David Langevin."

After arranging a meeting with David, Don gave me a crash course so I could fully understand the business functions of the other East Coast distributors, which performed functions similar to Eusco. With that valuable intelligence, we crafted a proposal to acquire Telelect East and flew to Terex's corporate headquarters in Connecticut for the meeting with David.

From the start, I hit it off with David because he had tried years earlier to do a deal with Triarc and didn't get past the front door. David couldn't believe I had conducted business with Triarc and was on a first-name basis with the entire group there. It also didn't hurt that I owned Wright & Lopez, which had more than six hundred vehicles with the same equipment installed on them as the company Terex had just acquired.

"Let me buy Telelect East from you," I said to David. "Don and I will restructure it and put your national distribution network at ease."

I knew that alleviating concerns these distributors had about being cut off by the new owners of Telelect East would be a strong selling point. It would be a signal to other distributors like Eusco covering the remaining parts of the United States that Terex wasn't interested in final-stage assembly, and that meant job security for the remaining distributors.

"That's an interesting approach," David responded, suggesting we go to lunch to discuss the possibility further.

As we settled in at a restaurant, he got back to business.

"We like your proposal, but things are not as bad as you indicated in a number of areas," David said. He was referring to my consistent opinion about how tough this industry is to break into, especially given the abundance of second and even third generation ownerships.

"If everything is so good, perhaps you should just keep Telelect East and go talk with someone else," I said softly, trying not to irritate him too much.

"We're interested in your deal, Jim. You and I both know you would not be sitting here otherwise," he replied in an almost conciliatory tone.

Although we each had put a figure on the table, we were quite a ways apart on the selling price. If we hit upon an amount we could both live with, I felt sure we could complete the deal.

"Well, David, you know I'm going to go for a low number and you are going to go for a high number. Let's split the difference and be done with it," I said casually.

He put his hand out, said "okay," and we shook hands.

"Do you want to close fast?" I asked.

"Yes."

"We will close within forty-five days or possibly sooner if both sides are responsive to each other as we both prepare the necessary documentation."

As Don and I headed back to the airport, he asked, "What do you think our chances are of getting the deal?"

"What are you talking about?"

"What are our chances of actually getting this baby closed as our letter proposed?" he said with a little more clarity.

"We got the deal. It's done."

"What are you talking about?"

"Didn't you see us shake hands in the restaurant?"

"I thought that was saying we're on the right track."

"No. We will have our lawyer take our proposal and turn it into a letter of intent, saying we will close in forty-five days."

"Do you mean he agreed to let us have it all?" Don asked excitedly. "Gosh, Jim, this could be worth millions."

"Yes, it could."

"Neither of us thought we'd get a deal done this fast. What are we going to do about ownership?"

"What do you think of fifty-fifty?" I proposed. "You run it and I'll be the deal guy."

Don quickly agreed.

I didn't realize it at the time, but by suggesting my role as "the deal guy," I had finally hit upon what I wanted to be when I grew up.

Turning Point

All my previous experiences and self-education converged into one epic "ah-ha" moment:

Being a deal guy was what I was born to do. For years, I thought I was simply wandering from one idea or business enterprise to the next. It often bothered me that I wasn't working some master plan I had created early in life. I failed at HVAC repair work, succeeded at train car manufacturing, won big as an HVAC marketing rep, blew a few small business opportunities, bombed out when I tried my own metal fabrication business, and then hit my stride in the acquisitions business. Suddenly, "I got it": I didn't have a master plan, but God did. He'd worked through my failures, fits, and starts to put me together the way He wanted me. All I had to do was stay the course and take whatever next step needed taking.

Taking a Global Turn

There was no doubt about it: The acquisition bug had bitten me, big-time.

When Don told me, "I feel like I've trained my whole life for Telelect East," I understood exactly what he meant. I felt as if I had trained my whole life to be a deal maker. But becoming a full-time deal guy would have to wait. There was much to be done with Telelect East while simultaneously running Wright & Lopez.

With any acquisition, the inside management team can be vitally helpful to the incoming buyer. In our case, we received invaluable assistance from Kevin Kennedy, who one day would become the "K" in my company, KPAC Solutions.

As Telelect East's controller, Kevin had extensive knowledge of financial and operational issues. During the acquisition,

Kevin contacted customers to make sure Telelect East remained on their pay list and to ensure the company was paid promptly. Without his proactive efforts, a number of customers might have taken longer to pay their invoices, which of course would have adversely affected our cash flow. One of the most ethical people I have ever met, Kevin was also incredibly efficient. Don and I were beneficiaries of his hard work in the months leading up to the final closing of our Telelect East acquisition.

In addition, Kevin was familiar with the important industry events Telelect East attended each year, and he notified us of deposit deadlines for booth space at trade shows that otherwise would have fallen through the cracks. Kevin offered skillful guidance throughout the transition and in day-to-day operations.

Don and I worked closely as well. We communicated nearly every day, and each month we reviewed the Telelect East financials together and made adjustments as needed. Once the acquisition was complete, Don did a masterful job of managing the company and making it profitable, with Kevin serving as his right-hand man.

With Telelect East in capable hands and as sole owner of Wright & Lopez, I began looking for new strategic acquisitions either to broaden Wright & Lopez's geographical footprint or to expand its services into new applications, such as fiber optics. Either way, I wanted to continue growing.

In order to identify competitors and potential avenues of growth, I directed the managers of the largest operations within our nine-state area to undertake market research and competitive analysis. I also retained investment bankers with industry expertise, piggy-backed on their market research to determine the profit margins in potential areas of growth, and analyzed year-over-year growth in various segments.

My efforts to identify expansion markets and opportunities within the telecommunications construction industry led me down a number of paths, including traffic control devices, cable television, and cellular and traditional phone lines. I first identified cities with strong growth. Then I learned as much as possible about the target through Dun & Bradstreet reports. I also looked for useful information from the investment banking community and anyone else I could find with relevant information about companies doing related work. Finally, I visited each city to size up the competition in person.

When dealing with municipalities, it is important to keep in mind the direction in which a city is growing. That is where you can expect expansion in basic utilities. Infrastructure such as water, sewer, phone, and cable TV lines have to be added or rebuilt for increased capacity in a city's growth areas.

I discovered that the choices for expansion were not clear cut and were by no means guaranteed to be successful. In fact, it was expensive and risky to pursue acquiring competitors because many of the companies did not want to sell, while others wanting to sell asked a much higher price than I was willing to pay.

Acquiring an ongoing business is not easy for the buyer or the seller. Both sides must be committed to the process and willing to spend some of their own money to complete the transaction. The saying, "You have to kiss a lot of frogs to find a prince" may or may not be true for romance, but it is certainly true when hunting for an acquisition which results in two companies becoming one.

After evaluating dozens of potential acquisitions over a three-year period, I finally purchased Black Industries, a privately held telecommunications construction and maintenance company. At one time, Black Industries was publicly traded, and during its colorful history, it wound up in the hands of an intriguing character named Marty who resided in the Cayman Islands.

When I began negotiating with Marty, he would fly from the Cayman Islands to meet with me in the Miami airport. Marty was always tanned and dressed appropriately for someone living on a "paradise island," wearing slacks and slip-on loafers without socks. Both of our attorneys knew what we were up to, but for the most part, they stayed in the background.

As we zeroed in on a price, Marty told me, "You're getting a real bargain with this company."

I thought I was, too, because the company's track record was well documented, and I believed it had great potential. We settled on a purchase price of $3 million, which included some limited liabilities besides the traditional accounts payable.

For financing, I turned to a company called Sirrom Capital, largely because Charlie Ogburn had raised a lot of money for Sirrom. When I called Charlie about my interest in Black Industries, he arranged a conference call with Rob, Sirrom's vice president of marketing.

"I have a good friend here; our relationship goes back several years...," Charlie said as he introduced me by phone.

In a response reminiscent of the Triarc deal, Rob said, "If Ogburn is saying that about you, I can tell you right now we want to do business with you." As we made financing arrangements, we all realized the equity kicker (a provision that allows a lending party to increase its return above the interest rate charged to the borrower) was going to be the deciding factor for Sirrom. An equity kicker is most commonly used when the borrowing party would otherwise struggle with a high interest rate in the beginning years of the loan. By this strategy, the lender charges a lower interest rate—sometimes even below the Fed's rate—with possible rate increases over a set period of time.

For my deal with Marty, Sirrom received a warrant/option giving it the right to purchase for a dollar 10 percent of my company, Patton Management Corporation (PMC) . This option would be exercised only on the day that we sold PMC to shield Sirrom from exposure to potential lawsuits prior to the deal closing.

Sirrom's investment strategy was to look for companies like ours making strategic acquisitions and then make an initial public offering (IPO) of the purchased business. At that time it would exercise its 10 percent purchase option. Sirrom borrowed money for itself at a low rate and loaned it out at a higher rate. Its business model was made possible by the government's Small Business Loans Division. Historically, the U.S. government has recognized that a significant amount of new job growth comes from small businesses, and this loan program helps facilitate job growth through loans partially subsidized by Uncle Sam.

Shortly after our phone conversation, Rob visited my Atlanta office. He met my chief financial officer and me in our conference room, where, with Theresa's help, we had decorated the office to make us appear big and financially strong. This approach nearly backfired on us in the meantime, when a couple of potential customers from New Jersey met with us after we submitted a proposal to do some work for their company.

"Nice digs," one of them said admiringly. "We would never use you because we can see you're too expensive," he said wryly. Although we later got work from them, at the time I wasn't sure he was joking, and it taught me a lesson about the pitfalls of appearing extravagant.

Patton Principle 36

Don't second-guess yourself, be yourself. Trying to impress others because you think they think you should be different than you really are is a frustrating mind-game and usually doesn't accomplish what you hope for. "To thine own self be true" still works best.

Fortunately, Rob was pleased with what he saw and heard. After a few minutes of reviewing the Black Industries financials he said simply, "If you need $3 million, you've got it." Although Rob still had to go through the formality of presenting the deal to Sirrom's loan committee, his commitment to us was essentially a commitment from the bank.

After obtaining the acquisition funds from Sirrom, we set a closing date for Black Industries. When buying from a foreign entity, the IRS holds the acquiring company liable for any outstanding tax owed by the seller to the U.S. government for that specific transaction the buyer is consummating. Before writing a check to the seller, a smart buyer will pay the seller only after confirming that the seller's taxes are wired to the IRS at closing.

In the process of validating Marty's ownership and determining tax consequences, we were shocked to discover that he did not own Black Industries. He had fraudulently misrepresented himself, and the real owners turned out to be a wealthy family in the United Kingdom. Although the owners had retained him to handle management responsibilities, they were so hands-off that Marty had even convinced the Black Industry employees that he owned the company.

By the time of this strange discovery, we had already spent a lot of the money we borrowed from Sirrom in legal fees and other costs. The loan itself cost $100,000 to close. In addition, we had invested months in this deal and spent a lot of time traveling to Raleigh, North Carolina, where Black Industries was located. When we uncovered the scam, we began a frantic search to locate the true owners.

After tracking down the British family, I called the only number I had for them and spoke with one of the family members. As I explained the situation, it became apparent he wasn't aware of what Marty had been up to, but I got the impression that Marty may have been part of the family.

"Please forgive me," he said in a heavy British accent, "but you're hitting me with an awful lot here."

After providing additional details, I eventually got around to asking if he would be interested in selling Black Industries.

"What's the price?" he asked.

"Three million U.S. dollars," I replied, holding my breath as I waited for a response.

He replied that he would like to discuss the offer with the other family members and get back with me. About an hour later, he called and simply said, "Well, that price seems fair to us. We'll take it."

My lawyer and I looked at each other and said, "This can't be true." It was too much like a movie. We contacted the IRS, outlined the transaction, and gave them the names of the real owners.

"What do your records show? Have they been paying their taxes?" we asked, still uneasy, our deal hanging by a thread.

"These people do owe us some money," the IRS agent said rather pointedly.

"How much?"

"Twelve million dollars."

"We have a $3 million check here – what should we do?"

"Send it to us."

"We can't do that without the family's permission."

"We have a written agreement with this family that any assets sold will go to us to pay down their obligation."

We sent the check to the IRS, and the assets passed to us free and clear.

Marty apparently got suspicious and stopped returning our phone calls. For all I know, he is still fleecing people from a sun-drenched Caribbean island between tanning sessions at the beach.

After successfully integrating Black Industries into Wright & Lopez, the company grew solid enough to become an attractive acquisition target. I eventually sold PMC, the parent of Wright & Lopez and Black Industries, to a competitor. Able Telecom, a publicly traded company in Canada, bought us out for a multiple of the company's annual cash flow.

The sale was another turning point in my life because I realized the potential for repeating this process and making handsome profits along the way. By taking Wright & Lopez from a position of negative to positive cash flow, and shaping it into a stronger, more diversified company through the addition of Black Industries, our employees and I revived and grew it into a major player.

Meanwhile, Telelect East had been growing through the addition of a service center in Atlanta and one outside of Tampa. We also acquired a company out of bankruptcy that did the same type of work. Revenues more than doubled, and our profits also increased, making the business far more valuable than when we purchased it in 1997.

At the time Don and I acquired Telelect East, the company had two manufacturing plants. One was located in Glenn Allen, on the northern outskirts of Richmond, Virginia, and the other in Emmaus, Pennsylvania. Although these two facilities were part of the same company, the cultures were much different. The main difference was unionization. The workers at the Emmaus plant were part of the Teamster's Union while the Glenn Allen workers were non-union. This created a stark contrast in the way the two plants operated, but everyone tried to ignore "the elephant in the living room" and get along as well as possible.

When Don and I came on the scene, we quickly picked up the underlying tension between the plants. Productivity was not what it should be, and something needed to be done sooner rather than later. Kevin Kennedy once again proved himself invaluable by helping us evaluate strategies we could use to turn things around.

Of all our ideas, we assumed the longest shot was to get rid of the union altogether. Everyone liked the idea but didn't think it had much chance of happening. Yet after reviewing the union contract, the possibility became more plausible, and we decided to try booting the union out. What did we have to lose, we thought?

Before following the rules for the process to officially remove or "decertify" the union, we held a meeting with the workers.

Don, our senior partner by age, was clearly the best speaker and also the most well known to the employees. We chose him to do the talking. Our game plan centered on explaining to the workers what the union cost each of them and what they were (or weren't) getting for their money. Don's speech went straight to the compensation point.

"Why would you pay your hard-earned money each month for something you are not even using?" he asked, as all eyes and ears tuned in to him. "Do you realize there were only two grievances all last year? Both of them were submitted by an employee who doesn't even work here any longer."

Don poured it on, and at the end of his fifteen-minute talk, the shop employees were nodding their heads in agreement. When the decertification move was put to a vote, the union was out. The union was decertified, and the monthly deductions went back into the workers' pockets. In the end, we were surprised at how little the union resisted our plan.

Patton Principle **37** **If it's the most promising strategy, give the long shot a shot.** Sometimes the best approach to a problem seems like an impossibility—and it might be. But if you give up before you try, it definitely won't happen. You can always settle for second best later if your first choice doesn't pan out.

Although the union no longer existed, the union mentality, unfortunately, was still alive and well among many of the employees. Unlike the non-union plant in Glenn Allen, teamwork and cooperation were practically non-existent in Emmaus. No matter how much Kevin, Don, or the shop management tried to motivate workers, the Emmaus plant just couldn't compete with the Glenn Allen employees.

None of us wanted to close either of the plants, but we simply didn't have enough capacity to keep both facilities operating. So, rather than making the seemingly arbitrary move of selecting which plant to close, we decided to let the workers make the decision for us by having a contest between the plants.

To avoid giving either plant an advantage, we selected a customer's purchase order for two identical aerial platforms (also known as cherry pickers) and let each plant fill the order. This provided an objective way to measure which plant had the best productivity and the fewest quality issues. We told the employees at both plants we were going to do this as a test of performance and productivity. Although the management had debated whether or not to keep the test a secret so everyone would work at a normal pace, we finally liked the idea of getting the best effort from both plants.

Test day arrived, and we turned the facilities loose on the fabrication, assembly, and final operating inspection of the platforms. Although it was never stated, everyone knew the winner of this competition would remain open, and the losing plant would be closed.

When the production was complete, Glenn Allen won, hands down. Not only was the non-union plant able to produce the unit in fewer man hours, but the quality of its work was superior as well. Not long after, we shut down the Emmaus plant. I have often thought this would be a good study case for a university class. Even though the Emmaus plant voted the union out and was given an equal chance at success, the union mentality and culture remained, to the detriment of the workers.

Now: fast forward a few years. Telelect East had expanded to more than twice its size since Don and I bought it, and the company had become a major player in the industry. At that point, Terex decided it wanted Telelect East back.

During the five years we owned Telelect East, the electric utility industry had changed its strategy. The result was that companies such as Duke Power decided to increase the size of their territories. Naturally, the electric utility industry wanted the contractors that supported these utilities to manage a larger territory as well.

Terex then realized the need to expand the footprint of distributors like us, and it was large and strong enough to cover virtually any sized footprint. Moreover, Terex recognized a golden opportunity to get back into the final-stage assembly business and have a national reach that any electric utility would find advantageous. For Don and me, the trend came at a fantastic time. We had grown Telelect East as big as we could on our own and were ready to sell it. So after owning it for five years, we sold it back to Terex for a handsome profit.

Over the years, I've learned that timing is a critical aspect of success in deal making. Just as a savvy investor buys stock low and sells it high, private-equity buyers strive to purchase companies at a rock-bottom price and later sell for a profit.

In addition to favorable timing, there are five areas crucial to success in an acquisition: the customer base, operations, finance, legal, and information technology.

Just as a bride and groom inherit their in-laws, an acquiring company also inherits its customers. To have a chance of reviving a failing company, it is essential that the customer base be on solid financial footing. An ideal customer is focused, well managed, and financially sound, with management which adheres to long-term strategies and avoids vacillating from one idea to another.

One way to get a feel for a potential acquisition's customer base is to contact associations to which they belong. It's surprising how much information these associations will provide through a simple phone call, especially if the association considers the caller a prospect for membership. Internet searches, Dun & Bradstreet, and Dow Jones also are useful tools for evaluating customers.

Although a buyer has no control over the company's existing customer base, the buyer does control who will handle the other four critical areas. In the early days, I wore a number of hats, but as my acquisitions grew in number and complexity I realized I needed a team of experts to help me with each aspect of the business.

On the operations side, a company needs at least one strong leader or visionary—usually the company president. Depending on the business's size and number of locations, there also may be a general manager who reports to the president. Above the president, there may be a chief operating officer (COO)—normally the president reports directly to the COO—although sometimes the president is also the COO.

As we completed more deals, our experience made it easier to determine how to structure a leadership team in any newly acquired company. I had the pleasure of learning from some talented operations guys such as Rick Boyle, Kevin Kennedy, and Don Eden. When it comes to focusing solely on restructuring issues, though, the best restructuring manager I've known is Fil Filipov—the guy who fired my friend and Telelect East partner. Fil is a world-class operator who has restructured both private and public companies. At times in his career, he had more than a billion dollars in revenue-line companies reporting to him.

Simply by walking through a manufacturing complex—large or small—Fil can spot what is right and what is wrong, and develop in his head a restructuring plan which would take most people months to complete. He speaks five languages and is a seasoned global operations manager who knows exactly what to do and when to do it in restructuring a company. And although Fil has been a long-term friend and colleague, we didn't start off on the best of terms.

I first encountered Fil's savvy back when Don and I were negotiating with Terex for Telelect East. We didn't realize Fil was calling all the shots behind the scenes. He was a trusted member of Terex's senior management and reported directly to the CEO. Years later, Fil and I would laugh, argue, and debate the valuation of Telelect East versus what Don and I paid for it. But during the negotiations, we were intense competitors.

Don and I later learned from David Langevin that he and Fil were persuaded to sell Telelect East to us because of the speed at which we could close the deal and because we were willing to acquire the company's entire market area. Other offers Terex received had excluded certain states and/or cities, which meant Terex would have to engage in multiple negotiations and closings instead of just one. In what became a model for future KPAC acquisitions, we required only a fraction of the usual warrants and representations a seller normally would have to make with a buyer. In short, we made it easy to do business with us.

Patton Principle

38

Life is hard enough, so make it easy for customers to do business with you.

Continually ask yourself, "If I were my customer, how would I want me to do business with them?" Then do it.

Soon after the original acquisition of Telelect East, we participated in a conference call with Fil and the other eight distributors from various parts of the country. Ironically, Don was back in the position he held at Telelect East before Fil fired him. By that time in my career, I had knocked heads with hard-nosed guys like Fil and knew the call was likely to generate some heat based on what I was planning to say.

I prepared Don for potential fireworks, telling him that people like Fil need to have respect for us. Otherwise, he would simply chew us up and reduce us to scrap metal. I had a plan to get some respect from him in a very non-traditional (and, in hindsight, unbiblical) way. As soon as the call started and the fifteen or so people identified themselves, Fil began to talk about the lack of revenues and his displeasure with it. He was trying to pressure Don and me, as well as the other distributors, into generating more business which, of course, would translate into the distributors purchasing more platforms from Terex.

At that point, I loudly told Fil we needed Terex to spend money in a number of areas, including capital expenditures for new product offerings and quality improvements. I also mentioned the need for more timeliness in responses from the factory.

"Just who is that speaking?" Fil asked sternly, as I predicted.

Don started shaking his head left to right and lifted his tie up in the air as if it were a hanging noose.

"It's Jim Patton," I said, as I interrupted Fil time and time again, indirectly driving home the point that I didn't fear him. Fil kept his cool during the conversation, but I knew I had gotten his attention. From that day on, I was on his radar as one distributor who couldn't be pushed around.

I felt that if Don and I could get on a more level playing field with Fil, we might be able to develop a better working relationship with him rather than letting him dictate terms to us. Gradually, over a four- or five-year period, Fil and I began to trust and respect each other, and as I will explain in more detail later, he became the operations manager for KPAC Solutions' first international deal. After that, I would never make another European acquisition without him as my partner.

For any re-structuring, the position of chief financial officer (CFO) is critical, because any banking relationship is going to be highly dependent on day-to-day relations and communication with the CFO. A competent CFO also has a good relationship with outside auditors who produce a company's audited financial statements. A CFO's management of relationships is second only to the CEO.

Over the last two decades, I have experienced the extremes of working with a disaster of a CFO to one who is the cream of the crop: Robert (Bob) Gielow, KPAC's chief financial officer. Bob was born to be a CFO, and I cannot imagine doing another acquisition without him beside me. His talents dwell deep inside that huge brain of his, yet Bob is as polite, quiet, and humble a man as you will ever have the pleasure of meeting. His capacity to analyze financial data in a multitude of formats makes him so valuable I consider him irreplaceable.

Bob and I met years ago through one of my deals. After having him on my team and seeing his knowledge and experience at work, I would never want to go back to the "pre-Bob Gielow" days.

Patton Principle 39

Work with valuable people and then value them. Make sure the people who serve you well know how very much you appreciate what they do. The effort you invest in encouraging and honoring them will pay greater dividends—personally and financially—than anything else you do.

Good legal help in running a company is an essential part of the make-up. A full-time staff attorney is typically one of an organization's highest-paid positions, so while larger companies sometimes have internal legal counsel, the smaller the company the more likely it is to retain outside counsel for legal representation. I still use outside legal counsel and have yet to acquire a company with an attorney on staff.

I have found that there are two kinds of lawyers: deal breakers and deal makers. Michael Hinchion, a senior partner with Stites & Harbison, is one of the latter, and he has been a dream come true for me over the last decade. I met him when another attorney I was using had a conflict of interest on a particular transaction and recommended Michael. As with Bob Gielow, Michael has thoroughly earned my trust and carries a great deal of authority on my behalf. If he says "No," then "No" is the answer—no further questions, end of story. That's the way it should be with your legal people. And it's even better if, like Michael (a CPA and expert in tax law), your counsel is knowledgeable in accounting.

In today's world of Web-site hosting, conferencing capabilities, and worldwide computer link-ups, information technology (IT) personnel are vital.

As with legal services, small companies often contract out for IT support, while larger companies have an IT team on staff, headed by the information technology officer. KPAC Solutions uses an Eastern European firm called AM Studio to handle transitions from the seller's IT support system to KPAC's. Most often, we implement a stand-alone system for the acquired company. This complicated process is contingent on what the company produces and in what part of the world its manufacturing facilities are located.

The Internet has brought about major changes in how businesses communicate and operate. In 2007, for example, KPAC bought a business that operated globally, and at the time, its Web site was getting an average of forty hits a month. When we sold it on the last day of 2009, it was getting more than 50,000 hits a month, and over 80 percent of new sales were generated over the Internet. KPAC did little to make this happen other than spend money on IT infrastructure to allow the processing to take place.

As important as it is to have a capable team in place for domestic acquisitions, it becomes exponentially more important when buying a foreign entity. After successfully acquiring six distressed manufacturers from public companies, I hit upon an opportunity to make our first international acquisition.

James Burns International (JBI), a France-based subsidiary of U.S. owned Standex International Corporation (NYSE:SXI), produced a broad range of machines to punch holes in paper and insert a plastic or metal spiral binder. With a global market position, JBI was on Kinko's approved vendors list, meaning JBI equipment was authorized to be used in every Kinko's store worldwide as well as numerous other chain stores in the office supply industry.

In spite of this stupendous market position, the company's performance over the years was like a yo-yo. An NYSE public company, Standex had long wanted to remove JBI from the other portfolio companies it owned, which had solid earnings and good growth opportunities.

Although it might seem ironic that JBI's dominant global position was a negative for Standex, the reason is that having a heavyweight player in one particular industry limits growth opportunities for a public company as a whole. Standex liked JBI's two revenue streams—one from the sale of new machines and the other from residual revenue of selling spiral binders— but the negatives outweighed the positives.

When Roger Fix (yes, "Fix" really is his last name) became president and CEO of Standex, he announced a restructuring plan he hoped would impress industry analysts and institutional stock owners alike. The subsidiary had become an albatross around the Standex corporate neck, and by now Standex just wanted to get rid of the company.

To handle the sale, Standex retained Seale & Associates, a global advisory firm with expertise in mergers and acquisitions. I had worked with Jim Seale, the firm's founder and president, on another transaction that turned out well for both of us, so when I learned that JBI was for sale, I submitted a proposal through Jim to buy it. Standex apparently wasn't impressed with my offer and told Jim to put it on the back burner, waiting to see what the marketplace said the company was worth.

Eight months later, I again contacted Jim to touch base on a few topics, one being JBI. Because of the confidentially involved in deals like this one, each company being considered is assigned a code name, and JBI was known as "Finisher."

"Did you ever sell that spiral printing machine deal, code-named Finisher?" I asked.

After a short pause Jim said, "Nope, it seems all roads lead to KPAC on this deal."

He agreed to re-submit our offer to Steve Brown, Standex's vice president of Corporate Development. The timing must have been just right, because shortly after, I received a call from Jim saying Standex would like to meet.

In terms of its size and revenues, JBI fit right in our "sweet spot" of targeted manufacturing companies. There was one major difference, however. Unlike previous KPAC acquisitions, JBI had five facilities in five countries: Sweden, Great Britain, Mexico, Singapore, and France. It also had a presence in New York, Georgia, and California.

Kevin Kennedy, by now a KPAC team member, had preliminary conversations with people who had the necessary background to manage the international pieces of the JBI deal for us, but Fil was by far my first choice. Having never bought a company outside of U.S. borders, I realized we needed someone who really understood how business is done internationally. Otherwise, acquiring JBI might backfire on us.

I had not talked to Fil about taking the CEO title and restructuring the entire company, but I thought he would be perfect for the job, given his track record of acquiring companies in Europe and the Far East. Although he had officially retired from Terex, I didn't think he would really stay retired for long. Fil is the crème de la crème in distressed manufacturing turnarounds, and many companies tried to hire him because of the instant credibility he adds to a management team. I was prepared to beg, if necessary, to get Fil to agree to help me with the JBI deal. Fil travels extensively, and I didn't know what part of the world he would be in so I just called his cell phone, hoping to reach him.

After the third ring he picked up and said in his usual manner of speaking, so softly I could barely hear him, "Fil Filipov." He was on a Nile River cruise ship.

"Hello Fil, this is Jim Patton," I said with more excitement than I intended to convey.

"Hey, Jim! What are you doing these days?"

Fil and I had learned that neither of us like to just chat on the phone, so I immediately got to the point of my call. I gave him a one minute overview of JBI, a quick rundown on Standex, and a briefing on how I got into the deal through Seale & Associates. After no more than five minutes, Fil asked me to FedEx "the book" to him.

The book is a documented story line of the company for sale. It gives a brief history of the company and specifics about the product it manufactures, followed by multiple years and interim audited financial statements. The book is normally thirty-five to fifty pages long.

Usually, the book is sent to multiple financial and strategic buyers with the intention of attracting at least two prospective buyers. That way the seller hopes to achieve the highest valuation possible. The process can take six months or more from the initial inquiry to the actual purchase of the company.

Sometimes, events or circumstances change within the company or industry, which require an explanation beyond what the book offers. If the additional information is not good news, communicating it to the potential buyer can be tricky and can make the valuation harder to justify, even if the new development is minor.

After reviewing the book, Fil sent an e-mail to me saying he was interested and asked what I was prepared to offer him. I put together a package which included salary, equity, and benefits commensurate with his expertise and with the size of the deal. The response I received has become his trademark way of acceptance: "Filipov is on board."

Drawing on Bob Gielow's financial analysis, Fil began an aggressive reorganization plan designed to make JBI profitable by becoming the low-cost producer. The binding industry was highly competitive, and profit margins were so thin many companies were going bankrupt. Fil planned to make the best product possible at the least expensive price. This necessitated closing some facilities, including two retail outlets which were big money losers. Previously, JBI used the outlets as expensive research and development labs, and we had calculated losses of about $1 million per year on those two outlets alone.

In addition, Fil reduced the number of product offerings (which ranged from machines that could bind one book at a time to ones able to handle hundreds of thousands of pages a week for items such as calendars). He limited the number of spiral-binding colors after discovering about 20 percent of the colors produced 80 percent of sales, and he developed new pricing and marketing strategies.

Through its new low-cost structure, JBI was able to sell profitably into a mature, stagnant marketplace. Under Fil's leadership, the company went from a net loss to making impressive profits in just two years.

Patton Principle

40 **When there's a way, find the will.** Often, the difference between those who achieve "the impossible"—like strong company growth in a stagnant market—is not just knowing how to make the necessary changes but having the determination to follow through and get it done.

Through the JBI experience, KPAC's transition from a U.S.-based private equity company tightly focused on manufacturing companies to a global company was accomplished much quicker than most people would have imagined—especially me! After completing our first cross-border transaction, we discovered there are not many private equity companies willing to do an international deal if the business has a valuation of under $40 million. Most prefer revenues in the hundreds of millions of dollars, and even then it would be difficult to find many potential acquirers.

In the following years, KPAC has had manufacturing plants operating concurrently in Europe, the United States, and Asia, a track record distinguishing KPAC from many larger private equity groups doing only U.S. deals. I had come a long way from my days of dabbling with small business to making large, intricate acquisitions of domestic companies. Now, the firm I started in 1991 had gone international, with manufacturing operations on three continents.

Like Dorothy, I knew I wasn't in Kansas anymore.

Turning Point

When the pieces fell together and KPAC came into its own, all the twists and turns in my career finally made sense.

In talking about the Lord's plan for our lives, it's almost a cliché to say, "God never wastes anything." When you finally see everything fit together, though, that truth is anything but trite. I had to sit back and just appreciate what He'd done in my life, and I still do. I realize we are supposed to "be thankful in all things," but it's easier sometimes than at others. When His blessings and gracious plans become obvious, take advantage of the natural inclination that will rise up within you to worship Him for who He is and what He's done for you. Blessing Him is a blessing for you.

Turning Wrong Turns
into Right Turns

As you see from my life story, my career has been riddled with mistakes, both large and small. And after running my own businesses for more than two decades, my list of what not to do just keeps growing. I'm okay with that, though, because the way I see it, making new mistakes means I am still learning. Thankfully, mistakes have been fewer and less costly after we formulated our current KPAC Solutions strategy.

Writer Rita Mae Brown observes, "Good judgment comes from experience, and often experience comes from bad judgment." For a long time, my primary teacher was pain, but as Rita Mae suggests, the pain which followed bad judgment has taught me a thing or two. I hope you will learn from my experiences and avoid making some of my mistakes.

While certainly not an exhaustive list of considerations when purchasing a business, the ten items detailed in this chapter come from many years of doing deals. Below each heading, I share a key question to ask yourself before you get out your checkbook and sign on the dotted line. At the end of the chapter, I include a couple of wrong turns I made and how you can avoid them.

#1: Know how to estimate cash flow and cash requirements.
Key question: How much money is it really going to take to operate this business?

This should be the number one item on any entrepreneur's list, as exemplified by my Mid-South experience. My partners and I purchased Mid-South without generating a meaningful analysis of the cash needed for running it. Instead, we agreed to use our lender's method of calculating how much money we needed to borrow. The business failed largely because: (1) I agreed to pay too much for the assets and (2) I let the bank push us around by lending less money than we truly needed. I've summarized below how to make sure that doesn't happen to you.

For an established manufacturing business, the easy formula in determining working capital required to run the business on a day-to-day basis is accounts receivable plus inventory, including work in process (WIP), minus accounts payable. Still, cash flow must be determined, and in the last fifteen years or so, EBITDA (Earnings Before Interest, Taxes, Depreciation and Amortization) has become a broader-based financial tool in the business and banking world. EBITDA defines "free cash flow," and it is common for lending institutions to include this calculation in both the commitment letter (used by the bank to show a potential borrower its interest in formalizing a loan) and the borrowing-base certificate (the worksheet a borrower fills out on a daily, weekly, or perhaps monthly basis depending on the level of comfort the bank has with the outstanding loan amount).

The bottom line is how comfortable the bank is with you and the loan amount requested.

Once the fundamentals are worked out, there are different methods of developing a forecasting spreadsheet. A good certified public accountant (CPA) can help create an appropriate forecasting model for your business. The nuances within a particular industry may affect the company's cash-flow requirements. For example, some industries are known for very long payment terms, while other industries require consignment of finished goods at the distribution level. This can deplete cash flow by having unsold inventory sitting at the end-customer's location.

Even the nature of materials used in a particular industry can affect cash flow. Consider, for instance, a company in an industry dealing with corrosive materials. The corrosiveness takes a toll on the equipment used to produce the company's products, thus requiring more frequent spending on capital improvements to replace the equipment. These issues need to be carefully evaluated prior to the acquisition or start-up.

#2: Be cautious about investing in a start-up business unless you are buying a franchise or have a wealth of personal experience within the industry.
Key question: What information do I need to evaluate the company?

An existing business can provide historical data, which reveals vital information for a new owner about its operations. It has been my experience that starting a new business requires roughly twice as much working capital and double the amount of time expected in order to achieve the beginning goals of the new business. Although this might be hard to believe, time and time again it has proven to be a good rule of thumb.

If the company is a start-up and not a franchise, almost everything has to be estimated—including mistakes!—but an existing business will have records which provide background data such as:

- Past financial performance and forecasting for one, two, or three years;
- Cyclical tendencies;
- Manpower allocations on monthly, quarterly, and annual basis;
- Month-to-month working capital needs;
- Capital expenditures needed each year, including a three-, five-, or seven-year analysis of equipment replacement;
- Property, plant, and equipment (PP&E) requirements;
- Historical benchmarks used for financial analysis of the specific industry.

#3: Determine your marketing strategy.

Key question: What is the company's market share, by product offering or service?

One of the first things to consider before getting involved in an existing or new business is how the company is, or should be, positioned in the marketplace. I suggest beginning this process with a market analysis which includes the company's actual or potential market share, its prospects for growth, and a thorough evaluation of the competition.

How to market the product is always an important long-term consideration. Unless the marketing strategy is already established, a manufacturer normally has two primary methods of market representation. One is to maintain an internal marketing team, and the other is to use a manufacturing representative— either a distributor which takes ownership of the product or an independent representative which sells from the company's inventory or which takes manufacturing orders. Depending on how well the product sells, the sales territory may expand or contract. Therefore, smart management will continually monitor sales patterns to make sure the territory (the existing or the potential customer base) is adequately covered at all times. It's also important to evaluate which advertising and public relations strategies are most effective in reaching the target audience and what those strategies will cost to implement.

#4: Identify the barriers to entry.

Key question: What will it cost me to get into this business and compete effectively?

Any obstacle which makes it difficult for a company to enter a new business and/or a new market is considered a barrier to entry. Control of resources, economies of scale, predatory pricing, strong competitor brands, and exclusive agreements with important distributors or retailers that already cover the market area are just a few examples of barriers which can make it difficult for a start-up to get into a specific industry and compete adequately.

Some barriers are intentionally created by existing companies to discourage competition from entering the market. These barriers should be carefully studied before getting involved with a business. You also should search for holes in the market you may be able to fill—such as segments not being served—and determine whether it is realistic and cost-effective to enter the fray.

One of my companies was in the earth-moving equipment business, and we developed and patented a new piece of equipment able to be used around the world. Each unit was the size of a large dining room, so it was no Tinkertoy. Even though we had ample manufacturing floor space, we started with a modest goal of completing two units a month.

While the market was receptive to our new product, our production capabilities were dependent upon how quickly we could produce the sub-assembly parts, weld all the components together, and then paint the unit. Eventually, we increased production to ten units a month, but by that time competition was hot on our heels with a similar product. Although we were the first to get an innovative product to market, our competitor capitalized on our slow assembly time, which allowed it to meet market demand with a rival product. Just because a product starts off as the leader doesn't ensure that it will stay the leader.

#5: Look for creative ways to do more with less.

Key question: How can we work smarter, not harder?

Making time to compare your company with your competitors may lead to some interesting findings. I once visited two plants performing the same function. One used nineteen people in a multi-step process to fill, seal, and transport fertilizer bags to an eighteen-wheel truck. The other plant needed only two.

How is that possible, you may ask?

The plant using two employees knew how to work smarter, not harder. The fill and seal functions were automated. Then, compressed air under a long transport table stretching from the end of the production line to the waiting freight truck, like an air-hockey table, created frictionless, efficient movement of the product. It moved fifty-pound fertilizer bags so an employee at one end merely pushed the bags across the table, and a second employee unloaded it at the other end. This is American ingenuity at its best.

#6: Investigate the specific management expertise and staffing needed within the business.

Key question: What resources do I need to run this business properly?

"Tribal knowledge" refers to what workers know that cannot be found on engineering prints or operations manuals. This knowledge comes from the day-to-day experience of actually producing the product, and it can provide shortcuts saving anywhere from minutes to hours on various tasks.

Without this vital component, starting a business means learning the hard way—also known as on-the-job training. While such training is appropriate for new employees, learning on the job can have disastrous consequences for a new owner. One way to get up to speed is to tap into the tribal knowledge of the company you are thinking about buying. Keep investigating and asking questions until you fully understand what it will take to manage the company profitably. It also helps to have someone on the management team you know and trust and who is well-versed in the industry.

In chapter six, I told about my partnership in a video rental business for grocery store chains. That story is a good example of a business I invested in without understanding one crucial piece of tribal knowledge. When I got involved in the business, I did not realize how much the types of movies customers wanted to rent was contingent on the store's geographical location and age of its customers. Had I studied each store's demographics and taken time to talk with each store manager about his or her customers, I would have had a much better picture of who shopped there and what types of videos would be most appealing to them.

Make sure you consider the unique staffing needs for your particular business, as well as the expertise needed to operate it. This includes asking if it is too top heavy with management. If it comes to trimming the workforce, though, tread carefully. Remember that every employee who walks out the door takes with him or her valuable tribal knowledge and experience.

#7: Consider the age of the business and industry.
Key question: How old is the industry, and what are the expected average profit margins?

A company which is a leader in a new industry typically generates larger profit margins than the competitors which follow. As a rule of thumb, the older the industry the smaller its profit margin. When a highly competitive industry ages, profit margins tend to shrink even as its product becomes faster and cheaper to produce. Although mobile phones are relatively new, for example, the industry is maturing, and mobile phones have become more common and less expensive. Laptop computers are another example of an aging industry. Be sure you understand where the business and industry are in their life cycle.

In a mature industry, such as home heating equipment, the units are expensive and designed to last for many years, and because of the cost, most people will make their heating equipment last as long as possible. When something breaks down, people usually try to get new parts rather than replace the entire unit.

Needs vary geographically as well. Some parts of the Northeast still use heating oil for furnaces in older homes. But in modern and newly constructed homes, more cost-effective alternatives, such as natural gas or propane, generally are used. In addition, oil furnaces require more maintenance than gas or propane, so when one breaks down it is unlikely the owner is going to buy another oil furnace. Considering the limited geographical market and the almost non-existent opportunities for growth, you would want to think long and hard about buying a company making oil furnaces or parts. If you buy into a declining market, you may be purchasing a dinosaur nearing extinction.

If you are considering a sub-assembler manufacturer, which makes a portion of a product and then ships it to the final assembler, it's especially important to understand where the industry is in its lifecycle. A sub-assembly part can be displaced in the market much easier than a complete product line, so if you acquire a sub-assembler, you are much more vulnerable to even the slightest industry change.

Introducing a new product or entering a new industry can create wonderful opportunities in yet-to-be defined geographical areas. To illustrate, suppose you are a franchisee in a new fast food franchise. When the franchise initially enters a state, you may be able to get rights to an entire city just by putting up one restaurant. After ten to twenty years into a successful franchise opportunity, though, market areas might be defined by streets within a city instead of the entire city.

#8: Determine whether the business is on the upswing or downswing.

Key question: Is this the right time to buy?

If you purchase a business during an upswing, you are likely to see revenues increase. Conversely, a business acquired on the downswing means smaller revenues and possibly softer margins. So ask yourself if this is the right time to venture into the market. Perhaps conditions will be more favorable in a year or two. Some businesses swing from the very best of times to the very worst in seven-year cycles. Other businesses have much shorter swings due to the age of the industry.

For example, as a business owner you wouldn't want to have an excessive inventory of flat-screen TVs because the industry is changing so fast. You could find yourself stuck with TVs that quickly become outdated and difficult to sell. On the other hand, if you own a company making telephone poles, these poles have remained virtually unchanged for decades, and you're not likely to have trouble with industry design trends. There was a time, not long ago, when typewriters were in great demand, but as word processors entered the market, typewriters became part of a dying industry. Now they are more likely to be found in a museum than in an office. More recently, e-mail has drastically reduced the number of faxes and letters companies send each day. And when was the last time you used a pay phone?

Some companies have proven themselves nimble and adaptable in rapidly-changing environments. Federal Express and UPS, for example, have staved off challenges from faxes and e-mail, and both companies continue to prosper. By contrast, the U.S. Postal Service continues to lose money, calculated in the billions of dollars per year as of this writing.

Another consideration is that new technology may generate a re-birth within an industry. A good example is the printed circuit board industry. KPAC owns a manufacturer of drill bits, which are used to make tiny, but high-precision holes in circuit boards. Micro computer chips are then installed in those holes. A circuit board could have more than twenty thousand holes drilled in it, and as new chips with greater computing speeds hit the market, the entire board has to be re-designed to accommodate them. This greatly increased the demand for our drill bits.

#9: Know what you're buying.
Key question: Have I fully investigated and evaluated all the company's assets and liabilities?

When my partner and I bought Wright & Lopez, a two-story storage facility was part of the package. The building housed a remote telephone distribution hub for equipment and extra supply parts and equipment. A huge antique safe was among the "equipment," and it had resided on the second floor for more than fifty years—ever since the building was constructed. One weekend thieves broke into the building and tried to remove the safe. They managed to move the safe to the first level where they cut holes in the floor. Because of the safe's size, however, they still couldn't get it out of the building. Their solution? They set the building on fire to cover their tracks.

Fortunately, we had replacement insurance for the building and its contents, which were far more valuable than any of us had realized. Until the fire, we did not know our transformers—which were collecting dust on shelves—had large amounts of silver in them. The insurance company had to replace those transformers at a cost of more than $100,000, due largely to the silver content.

While this incident literally had a silver lining to it, I learned the importance not only of having good insurance coverage, but also of knowing the value of assets that may not at first seem especially valuable. In this instance, underestimating the worth of my assets worked to my advantage, but just the opposite was the case at Mid-South where the assets were overvalued. The lesson is to know what you own and its true worth.

Corporate legal structure is also an important consideration in a potential acquisition. From a tax standpoint, it matters very much whether a business is a corporation or Limited Liability Company (LLC). If the company is not an LLC, there are two possibilities: a C Corporation or an S Corporation. In either case, a vital tax point to remember is this: If you have multiple S's under your ownership, you can deduct the annual loss of one S against the annual gain of another. However, you cannot do that if you own one company that is an S Corporation while the other is a C Corporation. This is critical when you first look at valuations issues and the year-after-year consequences of ownership. A good tax attorney can advise you on this issue.

#10: Never, ever assume you know what the customer wants.

Key question: Is there a viable market for the company's product or service?

In two of my turnaround ventures, I did not seek out the customers' desires at a time the companies were considering new ways to generate revenue. I simply assumed the customers would want our new offering, and both efforts ended in miserable failure. Our companies survived but at a much greater cost than was necessary.

Students in introductory marketing classes are taught the importance of market research, yet for entrepreneurs on a budget it can be tempting to try to save money by making educated guesses about what customers want rather than investing in research. But believe me, it's far more expensive to make assumptions that later prove to be wrong than it is to spend some money up front to determine whether there really is a market for your product or service.

Two Wrong Turns

I mentioned there were two business acquisitions for which I violated this principle. One was a telephone construction company, and the other was a wholesale wood supplier. Both involved some of my career's "wrong turns."

The telecommunications construction company had more than six hundred employees in the field as well as additional support personnel. At the time, the cell phone industry was booming, and we created crews whose specialty was installing cellular towers. Our parent company formed an LLC called TEAM, which stood for Tower Erection And Maintenance. We hoped to eventually spin-off the cellular business to a strategic partner or to a utility that was interested in having in-house capabilities.

My strategy was to get permission from railroads to erect towers on their right-of-ways through every major town and city in the nation. The process we had to go through to obtain permission from the railroad industry became much more expensive and time consuming than I ever dreamed, but the prospect of building a company I could take public lured me.

I also was encouraged because the cable television industry announced it was exploring ways to use fiber optic networks as infrastructure for cellular expansion. My partners and I were so convinced we had a winning concept that we executed confidentiality agreements to protect our idea and the way in which we gained railroad right-of-ways.

I fixated on this tower opportunity and started pushing as hard as I could to get approval from the railroad's safety board. Unfortunately, railroad management moved like its freight trains: steady but slowly. Our engineering drawings required approval by layers and layers of management, and the railroad leadership was concerned about where the towers would land in case some of them fell. As a result, their engineers got involved in the design and dragged out the process even further.

As our planning with the railroads crept along, our expenses mounted. We spent hundreds of thousands of dollars in engineering drawings alone before getting the necessary approvals. And nearly every city and subdivision was saying, "Not in my backyard" because they thought the cellular towers were too big and ugly for their neighborhoods.

We finally arranged a presentation to a major telephone company with a strong national focus on cellular communications. The meeting was in Texas, which involved another set of plane tickets, presentation materials, hotel expenses, and rental cars. It was one of many expensive trips for which my company had to pay.

When the big day arrived, we presented our idea of building cellular towers on either side of the railroad lines. It was brilliant, of course, since every city had railroad tracks running through it. We explained our vision with great enthusiasm, showing that railroad tracks everywhere had right-of-ways to allow for expansion or other needs—such as communications towers!

It was clear the company's upper management liked our idea. In fact, they loved it. But it had one devastating flaw: the timing wouldn't work. Telephone companies had already put together nearly 80 percent of the coverage they needed, and although their approach was more expensive than ours, they had already committed themselves, and it was too late for them to reconsider.

You could have knocked me over with a feather. My heart sank as the grim reality hit me that a year's worth of work and six figures in due-diligence expenses had just gone down the drain. That was it. The meeting was over, and out the door we went without an order. The same thing happened at every other phone company with which we met—great idea, but we were too late. The only things we had to show for all the work and money we spent over a year's time were expense reports and vouchers.

So what was the lesson? Ask the customer first what he or she wants before going too far down a path that will lead you nowhere! Just because something is a good idea doesn't mean it will sell. There has to be a perceived need for it, and the timing must be right. You can only determine those things through market research. Had we done our homework prior to investing so much time and money, we would have discovered that the telephone companies were just starting down this path, and we may have convinced them to switch strategies at this earlier stage. Or we may have discovered they just didn't have a need for the coverage we offered.

My second wrong-turn example involves a small wholesale wood import business in Atlanta. I purchased a controlling interest and had two partners. The first partner had worked inside the business, so I felt good about having covered the tribal knowledge aspect. The second partner was a trusted colleague and an excellent manager.

The company sold individual sheets of plywood measuring four feet wide by eight feet long, with a thickness that varied from an eighth of an inch to several inches, depending on the type of wood and the manufacturing method used. A wholesaler, our company sold products to lumber yards, which in turn sold them to contractors or individual customers. It was a mature industry and as a result, not highly profitable. Our pre-tax profit margins were just 2 or 3 percent net of all costs.

I visited a couple of the major importers in New Orleans as well as ports in California and Augusta, Georgia, where each year, huge volumes of plywood were imported from around the world, some of which were very expensive due to the type of wood used in the fabrication process. After studying the business for a few months, I believed we could gain better margins by eliminating one or two middlemen in the long line of ownership. It also became apparent that the most profitable part of the chain was the saw mill processing.

As I explored the possibility of owning a saw mill, I discovered the margins were even better if one owned the forest lands themselves. This is known as a vertical integration strategy, which means you expand your business by buying or internally building the business so you supply yourself with the components needed to grow.

Here's a real-life example from a coal mine owner. After buying trucks to haul coal to the shipyard, he decided to buy the shipyard. Next, he purchased a ship to transport the coal overseas, and before long, he bought the seaport on the other side. Finally, he bought additional trucks to haul the coal from the seaport to his overseas customer, who used the coal to generate steam. This vertical integration strategy, which turned out to be worth many billions of dollars, gave him control of the entire distribution process.

As a result of seeing this and other successful vertical integration strategies work for companies, I started looking for forest lands I could either buy or for which I could enter into a long-term tolling arrangement with the owner. (In a tolling arrangement a lumber yard uses its resources to prepare and ship the lumber without ownership changing hands. The lumber yard simply charges a fee for its services.) At the time, Peru had the eighth-largest forest reserves in the world but exported only a fraction compared to other countries that had far less reserves for exporting. After making fifteen trips to Peru over a year and a half, I secured property rights to harvest vast amounts of virgin timber from an area of more than 10 million acres. But because of strict harvesting methods, called "sustainable forestry management services," this project cost us hundreds of thousands of dollars just to assemble and prepare for cutting timber.

At the end of this costly venture, the fatal problem with my strategy emerged. My customers were not interested in paying any additional premium—no matter how small—for this superior timber. They simply did not see the value in it. I was shocked. Had it been up to me, I would have gladly paid a little more for these superior cuts, and I had assumed others would as well.

But then, I wasn't the customer, and as we all know, the customer is always right.

Learn from the Turns

People are often curious about what happened to Mid-South Tool & Die after I left, and the truth is, I don't know for sure. Although I never paid a formal visit, I drove by the facility a number of years after my stint of ownership, and the place appeared much like the first day I entered it: little to no activity.

I still feel a twinge of pain when I recall the trauma of losing Mid-South after investing so much of myself in it, but nearly twenty-five years later, I'm exceedingly grateful for all God taught me from that experience. As I mentioned earlier, one of the most important lessons is to never pay too much for a company, even if that means walking away from what seems to be an attractive opportunity.

When I look back on how the Lord lifted me up from the Mid-South ash heap to where He has brought me today, I can't help but echo what Paul wrote in 1 Corinthians 2:9: "...No eye has seen, no ear has heard, no mind has conceived what God has prepared for those who love Him."

With the benefit of hindsight, I can readily see the stupid mistakes I made when I first stepped into the business world. My ignorance of financial management in particular was the kiss of death in my efforts to resurrect Mid-South. One reason I'm thankful for the Mid-South debacle is that it changed my thinking and actions, which ultimately led to greater success than if I had somehow been able to keep Mid-South limping along.

But Mid-South was just one turn in my life. There have been many others, and in this final chapter I want to share with you what I consider to be the most important insights I've gained through my career. Some of these lessons came from hairpin turns. Other turns were made with the grace and finesse of a teenager learning to drive a stick shift. A few were long, looping turns which gradually transformed how I view life, business, and faith. The one thing my turns had in common was that each one changed me in some specific way.

Personal growth has been a major component of my life. I've been liberated by recognizing that some of the things I considered my greatest weaknesses—and which I feared people would find out about me—are now among my strengths. My lack of formal education, for instance, used to really bother me because I imagined people would look down on me if they knew I didn't have a college degree. But this perceived weakness constantly drove me to become self-educated in an attempt to fill the gaps in my business knowledge and acumen.

Moreover, early in my career I was reluctant to ask questions because again, I feared my lack of formal education would be exposed. Now, I consider asking questions a strength because I learn so much from the answers—or lack of answers—I get.

Ironically, my lack of education had an interesting unintended consequence: I found it can be a real advantage when others underestimate what you can do. Some of my most successful deals came about as a result of people underestimating me during negotiations.

Taking time to understand your own weaknesses is time well spent because you may find some of them can be turned into strengths. I've also come to understand that my significance and security do not depend on my next deal, but rather on my relationship with Jesus Christ. If my significance and peace are dependent upon how much money or power I acquire, I am indeed on shaky ground. Sooner or later, something in life comes along that neither money nor power can solve. Without a solid foundation in Christ, even a carefully built house of cards will eventually collapse.

Jesus asked one of the most profound and penetrating questions of all time: "For what does it profit a man to gain the whole world and forfeit his soul?" (Mark 8:36). For me, that question clarifies what is truly important in life.

As you know, it took awhile before what I believed about God was fully integrated into my business practices. I've shared examples of how I was rude to others, such as hanging up on Tom Howell, my future boss, and repeatedly interrupting Fil Filipov because I thought that approach would put me on even footing with him. I realize now that I succeeded in spite of, not because of, the poor way I handled these situations.

Then, of course, there are the times I moonlighted in a side business on company time and another occasion when I was not completely forthcoming on a business deal. I could share other failings, but the one piece of advice I would give anyone is to always follow the Golden Rule: Treat others as you would like to be treated. You absolutely cannot go wrong following this rule in your personal and professional life. I often wonder what a better example of Christ I could have been by more closely following biblical principles earlier on.

I could probably write a second book (hmm—maybe I will once this ink is dry) to adequately cover what I've learned from buying, running, and selling companies around the world. But I will conclude by sharing some general observations I hope will be practical and meaningful, regardless of what size business you have or are considering buying. These Ten Directives for Business will help you negotiate any turns you come to.

#1: Create an enduring brand for your company.

In the formative years, I changed our holding company's name with each new acquisition. This created a branding problem because there was no continuity in the company name. Recognizing this deficiency, I finally settled on a permanent name—KPAC Solutions—which I have used worldwide for nearly twelve years now. The lesson to be learned is to think beyond the immediate circumstances and visualize the company you want to have ten or twenty years down the road. Your brand can be a powerful asset, so start laying the foundation now.

#2: Pay attention to your competitors.

The competition never seems to rest, vacation, or take a sick day. Although they probably do, you should act like they don't. During my first successful business venture, I was busy pinching myself and enjoying the ride when I should have been more focused on running the business and studying my competitors. They were always out there trying to take some of my market share. I do believe that healthy competition is good, precisely because, one way or another, it destroys complacency. It keeps us on our toes, continually looking for ways to improve what we offer our customers.

#3: Make cost savings a priority.

Being the lowest cost producer can provide all kinds of advantages, such as improved cash flow, more effective material procurement, enhanced profit margins, and better inventory turns. The old "twenty-eighty rule" still applies in many cases: 20 percent of the product offering accounts for 80 percent of the profitability of the entire company. If the other 80 percent of the products aren't pulling their weight, it's worth giving serious consideration to either reducing production of them or discontinuing them altogether. There are lots of ways a business can save money if you are willing to objectively evaluate each expenditure.

#4: Treat employees fairly and with respect.

Good employees are worth their weight in gold. The best forecasting software can't compete with a plant manager who has decades of experience in a production factory. There are just too many nuanced variables that require a competent, confident manager to make tough, on-the-spot decisions inside a large and complex plant. Lots of companies say their employees are their greatest asset, but few really treat them that way. There are always exceptions, but as a general rule, if you treat your employees well and with respect, they will reward you with an honest day's work and more times than not make decisions that are in the company's best interest.

#5: Never take the last nickel lying on the table when negotiating a deal.

Long after the parties have left the conference room table, the agreement will live on. If either feels cheated, that last nickel will prove to be very expensive. Besides, someday the shoe may be on the other foot, and the opposing party will remember how well or poorly they were treated. Rest assured they will treat you like you treated them days, months, or even years later.

#6: Don't let a banker or a lawyer tell you how to run your business.

The big dog doesn't always get the same respect in the banking community as it does on the street. Market share is a banker's favorite way of determining who is the largest in a given industry, but it's not necessarily the best way to evaluate a business. Generally, the bigger a company, the more market share it holds. But the more market share a company enjoys, the harder it is for that company to grow. With 1 percent market share you can grow 100 percent by garnishing just an additional 1 percent of the market. But if you have a 50 percent market share, getting even an additional 10 percent is tough and doubling your share is virtually impossible.

Evaluation by market share is just one example of how bankers exert undue influence over a business. In my Mid-South days, I allowed a banker to reduce by a third the loan amount I really needed and then look over my shoulder daily by way of a lengthy and time consuming "borrowing base certificate" (which shows the outstanding loan balance and assets supporting it, along with other check points known as loan covenants)—usually to the detriment of the company.

Regardless of how large or small your business, you are in a better position to make management decisions than your banker or lawyer. They have certain expertise, and you should consider their advice, but they normally do not have the time to invest in seeing the big picture the way you do.

#7: Focus on what you do best.

One of the biggest lessons my failures have taught me is the importance of finding a niche and sticking with it. The acquisition strategy KPAC uses today focuses on acquiring companies with one or more of the following:

- An existing organizational structure with a direct industry link;

- Strong personal experience in KPAC that relates to the new business;
- End-users purchasing the company's products (not wholesalers);
- An operating partner who has solid industry experience.

Through our decades of combined experience, our team and I have developed a set of criteria for potential acquisitions that guide our decisions. We only buy financially distressed manufacturing companies, and while manufacturing covers a lot of territory, it's an industry we understand inside and out. We also stick to a certain range of revenues in the companies we consider.

Within seventy-two hours of receiving appropriate financial and operational information, we make a valuation and binding offer for a company that meets our criteria. With governmental approval, the average time it takes for us to close a deal is only thirty to forty-five days. We've even bought companies we hadn't seen operating or a division we didn't visit until a day or so before the scheduled closing. Why? Because we know what we're looking for and our experience enables us to conduct due diligence quickly and efficiently.

KPAC's prototypical seller is a Fortune 1000 company with an unprofitable subsidiary or division which it has failed to sell through the normal auction process via an investment banking firm or through the parent company's efforts to sell it. We bring an important component to the table, attractive to the seller— the certainty that we can close the deal quickly. The credibility we need to do this is supported by our unblemished track record, thus enabling the seller to get the money-losing business off its books in a matter of weeks.

When the transaction is complete, our team applies a plan to the newly acquired company that we call "One Hundred Days to Profitability." Then, once the company begins making money, we generally sell it within two to three years of the initial acquisition—often to an industry competitor—at a fair multiple of established earnings (EBITDA). Our average ownership period is twenty-six months, and KPAC has never had a failure or even filed for reorganization through bankruptcy for any company in which I owned at least 25 percent equity. We've discovered a formula for success, and we're not going to deviate from it, even if it takes years to find our next deal.

#8: Offer positive incentives.

In business, a negative incentive can be the kiss of death. Why would anyone pay employees less as they increase their respective sales or revenues? I'm happy to write big commission and performance checks, because the more I pay out, the more the company is making. Penalizing people for being successful simply does not make sense economically or morally.

I find it frustrating that both the federal and many state governments use negative incentives with our tax structures. The more someone makes the more that person's taxes increase. At a certain level of personal income, deductions, such as charitable contributions, are even eliminated. The final indignity is the "death tax." The after-tax dollars passed to the deceased's family through an estate are taxed again, even though the individual paid taxes when the money was first earned. Then the cycle repeats when the next generation dies.

While I believe paying taxes is part of the cost of being a free person and a citizen of the United States, excessive taxes on individuals and businesses will eventually kill the golden goose and undermine our nation's ability to compete globally. Just as I used to get nauseous flying over Birmingham when Wright & Lopez was losing so much money each month in its contract with BellSouth, I get that same sick feeling when I think about the staggering wastefulness of our government. America's tax system is broken, and I believe it needs a major overhaul to repair it. To accomplish that will require an "overhaul" in the way our elected officials have conducted themselves in the last fifteen or twenty years.

#9: Don't put off making hard decisions.

Unlike the federal government, companies can't stay in business and spend large sums of money when running a long-term deficit. Sometimes, a business owner must have the courage to make hard, unpopular decisions to keep the company going, because if the company goes under, everyone loses. It is not compassionate to run a business into the ground simply because you didn't have the heart to cut costs and eliminate duplicate or unprofitable jobs. At KPAC, our goal is always to save any manufacturing business we acquire and make it healthy.

Most of the companies we've purchased were on life support by the time we started running them, yet I'm pleased to note that we've never shut down a business entirely. We have closed plants and eliminated jobs, but only because those actions were absolutely necessary to keep the company afloat. By the time we have a distressed company up and running again, it's not unusual for us to have more employees than when we started. But even if we manage to save only forty-five out of a hundred jobs, if those jobs are stable and last for decades, I consider it worthwhile—and so do those forty-five workers!

A few years ago, Ralph Keller, president of the Association for Manufacturing Excellence in Arrington Heights, Illinois, told the *Nashville Business Journal*, "Companies like KPAC that are going in and fixing these broken companies are performing a service to the U.S. economy by preserving manufacturing jobs."

Whenever possible, we aim to save American jobs and make positive contributions to the economy. But that requires difficult choices and actions we sometimes wish we didn't have to take.

#10: Ask questions, and then ask some more questions.

Often, the second round of questions is created from the first round of answers the seller provides. In nearly every distressed company I've bought, the seller has asked, in one way or another, "What can you do that we haven't already done?"

I used to secretly fear that question, but not anymore. Now, I answer with questions of my own. By the time KPAC meets with a prospective seller, we have studied financials and understand the company's product mix, evaluated how products are sold and distributed, and learned how the organization is structured. With that knowledge in hand, we ask the seller pointed questions such as, "Why didn't you close the plant in x country when its capacity was clearly well below the break-even level, and it won't be above that level anytime soon?"

Or, "You seem to have duplicate personnel in your three plants. Why haven't you consolidated the organizational structure so you can manage the business more efficiently?"

Many times, we hear answers like, "Well, we knew we should have closed the plant, but we didn't want to send the wrong signal to the customer base. We thought we'd let the new buyer make that decision and handle the repercussions." In other words, they often know they're losing money through inefficient operations, but they want the tough decisions to be on someone else's watch. I've noticed, too, that this pattern seems to get worse as the parent company gets bigger.

Another situation we frequently encounter is a product line which obviously is outside the main focus of the company. This product line requires more attention than it deserves, because it serves only a small group of customers and is unprofitable. When we ask why the company hasn't divested itself of this money loser, a typical answer is something like, "This was one of the first products our company produced, and we didn't want to send the wrong signal in the marketplace by discontinuing it."

As outsiders, we look at a company objectively, rather than emotionally, which enables us to make the tough decisions. Yet I can certainly empathize with company insiders. I'm a good CEO for the first six months—until I get to know the employees. But once I start thinking emotionally rather than logically, my "No's" turn into "Maybe" or "Yes." A good manager will run a tight ship and continue to say "No" until he or she can see the business benefits of a particular course of action.

I once had an ownership interest in a Texas manufacturer of heavy earth-moving equipment for Caterpillar. Initially, we had to lay off quite a few employees, including some of the engineers. While they were wonderful, talented people, we just had too many of them. My partners and I determined we could make the facility profitable, though to do so we had to reduce the head count, limit our product offering, and find new customers. But first we had to deal with the company's union.

In both plants combined, the company employed more than six hundred people, and before we could make workforce reductions, the union contract required that we give the local union leaders seventy-two hours notice of our proposed changes. One change we intended to implement was requiring employees to multi-task rather than be limited to one activity. Unions, of course, like to limit the scope of an employee's job so the company has to hire more workers, which leads to overstaffing and decreased productivity.

Fortunately for us, the union agreement gave plenty of leeway for a new owner to make changes and restructure the company. Union leaders understood what needed to be done and were cooperative. They recognized that we were trying to avoid closing the company and liquidating its assets.

We eventually turned the company around and made it profitable. And after the first year, we not only called back employees we laid off, but also some that our predecessor had laid off. By the time I left the company, we had new work from an expanded customer base, sufficient to justify expanding the number of employees.

Of all the deals I've done, the letters I got from the employees of that Texas plant were the most complementary and grateful I've ever received. One reason we succeeded is that the union worked with us rather than against us, and it allowed management to focus on turning the company into a profitable operation able to sustain and eventually expand the workforce.

These Directives will work because they are based on rock-solid principles. But there's a very special reason they can work, and that I credit to the country I love and the founding principles of its republic and the economic vitality of its capitalistic system. Being able to freely follow these directives is why America remains, in my opinion, the best place in the world to do business. I've given a lot of thought as to why American business has thrived, and as I close this story, please give serious thought to my observations and suggestions about how we can once again make our nation's manufacturing industry competitive.

Epilogue

America's Good Turns:
The Case for Capitalism

One quality which has made America strong—and that we need to get back to—is an entrepreneurial spirit which flows from freedom. Historically, America's manufacturing capabilities have been the engine propelling our economy and helping to create a strong middle class. In Europe, I saw firsthand while living there that the middle class is now almost non-existent. There's little between lower and upper classes. In fact, most of the world is comprised of the "haves" and the "have-nots." The United States is clearly differentiated from the rest of world in terms of lifestyle and opportunities to excel, and these opportunities are available to all three of our economic classes: upper, middle, and lower.

As with the middle class, those at the lower end of the economic scale have the freedom to improve their circumstances and pursue the American dream. I'm living proof that America is the land of opportunity, for nowhere else in the world would my story have been possible.

During the Industrial Revolution and the decades that followed, each generation could do better than the previous one, but sadly, that is no longer the case. In the last ten to fifteen years, there has been such an erosion of America's manufacturing base that our middle class, in one generation, has lost what it took four generations to build. According to the Alliance for American Manufacturing, the U.S. has lost five million manufacturing jobs since 2000. And since 1999, more than 40,000 manufacturing facilities have closed as the sharp rise in global competition has taken its toll, and many jobs have moved overseas.

The middle-class dream is becoming a pipe dream. Unless we take action now to reverse this decline, the current generation won't do as well as their parents. Our children and grandchildren will be renters and remain in service-oriented jobs, while saddled with enormous government debt that can never be repaid.

We've also perpetrated a terrible injustice to those in the lower income bracket by creating a false sense of security through government entitlements such as food stamps and welfare. One of the results is an increase in single-parent families, often with multiple children from multiple fathers. Instead of lifting people from poverty and giving them opportunities to succeed, our welfare state perpetuates a cycle of government dependency and generational poverty.

In 1942, a Presbyterian minister named William J. H. Boetcker wrote, "You cannot help men permanently by doing for them what they can and should do for themselves."* His words are as true today as when he wrote them, and we would do well to heed what he says.

---

* http://www.quotationspage.com/quotes/William_J._H._Boetcker/

One way to solve some of our economic problems is to make a concerted effort to restore America's manufacturing capabilities. But first we need to learn from our past failures and understand the reasons we've lost so much of our manufacturing capacity to international competition.

When I was growing up, it was embarrassing to have something made in the Far East because it was considered "cheap." Now, just a few decades later, the Far East is not a joke anymore. Some of the world's biggest circuit board producers, for example, now are located in China.

America's ability to compete in manufacturing has been impeded by other countries' cheaper variable and fixed costs. The U.S. furniture industry, which for decades produced fine quality products, provides a good case in point. In the late 1990s, competition from China decimated the furniture manufacturing industry by offering a product of comparable quality, produced with a drastically lower labor cost. What's left is a dwindling base of domestic manufacturers.

I suspect there's nothing that can be done about getting that work back. Other industries, though, are facing similar pressures and challenges, and it may not be too late to help them. So what can be done?

I believe it's time to retool America and refocus on our strengths. To once again make America competitive in manufacturing, we have to start with a workforce that is educated, motivated, and willing to work in that sector. And just as a business owner must have the courage to discontinue products that lacking sufficient market share, we need to recognize there are some industries in which domestic manufacturers should not try to compete because they simply are not winnable.

America has inherent strengths. It is an open and free country that promotes free enterprise and that has enabled us to excel time and time again. This freedom sets us up for our greatest manufacturing strength: the ability to innovate. To make the most of this strength we need to identify new and profitable segments showcasing our innovation and competitiveness, while taking advantage of the skill sets we have in industries such as health care and engineering technologies. By gearing our efforts more toward technological advancements and sophisticated service industries, America can revive its flagging manufacturing capabilities. U.S manufacturers can produce precision components and replacements as well, if not better than, anyone else.

Additionally, there are opportunities for new health care products for disease treatment and management. Manufacturing these in the U.S. would be a boon for everyone from chemists to middle-class workers.

As difficult as it may seem, we also can compete with lower wages in other countries by identifying innovative ways to increase our productivity without compromising our standard of living. Remember the compressed air transport system in chapter eleven? Together with an automated control system, it reduced the number of workers needed from nineteen to two. If American manufacturers can produce ten parts as quickly as other countries produce one, they will regain a competitive edge through innovations which increase productivity even while we pay our workers significantly higher wages.

America also has unmatched expertise in developing weapons systems and aerospace technology. We sell billions of dollars in fighter jets and equipment to other nations, and we have strengths in the computer and satellite industries, both of which have excellent growth potential. We should expand our capabilities in those areas so that when a worker loses a job in another sector to competition overseas, we can re-employ him or her in an area where no one in the world can compete.

The government can support the re-making of American enterprise by realigning business incentives. For decades, foreign governments have offered incentives in the form of subsidies that give their companies unfair advantages over large

U.S. corporations that employ tens of thousands of workers. Communist nations in particular go to great lengths to limit the amount of market share American companies can gain in their countries by placing tariffs on imported goods. This imbalance is like a cancer eating its way through the economic fiber of America. The U.S. government should ensure that foreign competitors doing business in America pay similar tariffs in order to balance the playing field.

Our manufacturing base faces great challenges, but I firmly believe we can overcome them with the right strategies. American business has always confronted challenges, yet the free-enterprise system has proven resilient because of the unparalleled opportunities for success it provides to people in all walks of life.

While it is fashionable in some quarters to bash businesses of any size these days, "business" is what makes the country run. Most business people are honest, hardworking individuals, and their companies make important contributions to the economy and to society.

I have never understood people who have become successful through capitalism and now want to dismantle the very system that made their achievements possible. There is no equivalent to the "American dream" in Europe, Asia, or South America. Why would we want to deny future generations the opportunity to achieve their dreams?

If I had been insulated from failure, I would never have achieved my potential. If I had been stifled by excessive government bureaucracy, I would have remained shackled in mediocrity. And if I didn't have hope for a better life for my family and myself, my lifelong goal would have remained making twenty dollars an hour.

I'm convinced we learn more from our failures than our successes, but I never would have risked failure if there hadn't been a potential reward on the horizon. Killing off incentives to excel under the guise of homogenized fairness is killing off a part of who we are as Americans. It's in our DNA to reach for the stars.

The case for capitalism, as I see it, is simply that it gives every person an opportunity to pursue and achieve success, however that person defines it. Capitalism does not provide a guarantee of success, but it gives everyone an opportunity to try. When we fail, we learn from the experience, pick ourselves up, and try again. When we succeed, it not only improves our lot in life, but also provides us with the means to be generous to others.

As I wrap up my story, I can think of no more appropriate way to end than with Proverbs 3:5-6: "Trust in the Lord with all your heart, and lean not on your own understanding; in all your ways acknowledge him, and he will make your paths straight."

Many times, leaning on my own understanding proved disastrous, yet when I have acknowledged and trusted the Lord, He has indeed made my paths straight. One constant that has remained to this day is the Lord's perfect timing. Whenever one deal ended—whether through a purchase or sale—there has always been something else around the corner to provide for my family and my company. These are things I could not have foreseen or orchestrated; they were strictly the Lord providing for us each step along life's journey.

Allow me to leave you with a parting thought about your life in whatever turn lanes you come to. One reason a vehicle's windshield is so much larger than the rearview mirror is because drivers need to pay attention to where they're going, not to where they've been. I hope that by sharing my life's story you have seen a thing or two in my experiences that will be useful on your journey and help you make the right turns ahead.

Turn lanes are for changing direction, and I may yet have a few turns in the road I don't see yet. But wherever life's turns may lead the rest of my days, I know the One who is directing them. I'm also mindful that this world is passing away, and my real home and the destination of all my turns is heaven. I hope to see you there.

Appendix 1

The KPAC Solutions
Approach to Valuation

I f you're interested in pursuing an acquisition, this appendix explains KPAC Solutions' approach to valuing a distressed business. (We define a "distressed business" as one with a negative cash flow.) It relays some fairly technical information, but if you're ready to take the plunge, it will be well worth your time to review this section. Hopefully, it will help you avoid pitfalls such as the ones which proved so costly to me.

Because this appendix addresses only the valuation of distressed (as opposed to financially healthy) manufacturing companies, I recommend you also go through Appendix Two for a better understanding of the specific acquisition strategy employed by KPAC. Our extremely fast acquisition strategy has to assume many different things, the most important of which is that the financial statements have been audited by a very reputable firm.

Knowing the Financials

In case you didn't notice from my story, I'm passionate about the importance of using and understanding financial statements. If you're going to succeed in acquisitions, you must have a very good understanding of the financial statements by which businesses are measured, the records supporting them, and the way the various statements work together. The essential statements are:

1. **The balance sheet**, which compares all assets with all liabilities;
2. **The profit and loss statement**, which measures gross revenues (sometimes referred to as sales) to different levels of profitability, taking into account the taxes owed;
3. **The cash flow statement**, which illustrates the movement of cash in and out of the business.

I didn't have a solid understanding of these three documents until after the failure of my first significant deal. That's the deal into which I put all my money from savings, 401k plan, twelve years of profit sharing, and loans from family and friends. I also maxed out every credit card and, I admit, even dumped in money withheld for the IRS on behalf of my employees but not submitted (I ultimately became personally liable for those taxes as well). All my life's savings—and more—down the drain.

How could this terrible mistake happen, you might ask? Actually, it was quite easy to do—I just didn't pay attention to the financials.

I've summarized below the process I use when valuing a potential acquisition. Although the steps are numbered, they don't necessarily have to be done in this order. It's a checklist, and the important thing is to make sure you do all of the steps.

STEP 1
Make sure you understand and validate:

- The potential acquisition's fiscal year end—don't assume it is the calendar year end.
- The number of other companies represented in the consolidated statements.
- What type of corporation it is (S, C, or LLC—with many more possibilities if the acquisition is outside the United States).
- The difference between "book" (GAAP) verses "tax" (what has been filed with the IRS). GAAP stands for "Generally Accepted Accounting Principles", which are established guidelines for financial accounting.
- Whether or not there are revenues generated from a sister company with the same owner as the company you are looking at acquiring. (Under some circumstances, this could be a meaningful strategic alliance. Or it could be a complete disaster if you count on the continuation of that revenue, and the seller plans to immediately terminate those relationships. This falls under the heading of "eliminations" on the parent company's consolidated balance sheet.)

If the seller is a public company, it is important to read the most recent filings by quarter and last fiscal year-end reports. Make sure you get 100 percent clarity on any and all company eliminations on the consolidated financial statements.

STEP 2

Make sure you understand:

- Every single line description for all assets and liabilities. Get explanations of abbreviations, groups of letters only, or any other line-by-line description found on the financial statements.

- Make sure you fully understand any "adjustments", "add backs", or "normalizations" used in the production of the financial statements or projections. These terms usually mean some group or person—the seller's employees, management, and/or outside advisor or investment banker—makes an adjustment so the profitability seems better or makes an improvement to the balance sheet or cash flow statement to the benefit of the seller.

- Make sure you fully understand each sub-total line beyond the obvious. Ask: why did the seller put it there?

- Make sure you can match dollar for dollar (or whatever currency applies) the depreciation and amortization by line-item detail from the balance sheet. This will ensure the same amount of equipment is accounted for even if it was completely written off during the normal course of business and according to the correct depreciation schedule.

- Make sure you have three years of historical information and at least three years of annualized forecasting by month. Also, get the most current interim statements available, which normally should be ready for release by the fifteenth of the following month.

Remember: There are two sides to the balance sheet, so make sure you process both the liabilities side and the assets side.

Step 3

Develop a "Sources & Uses" comparison chart early in the valuation process.

In this chart, demonstrate where the different potential sources of the purchase price are going to come from. The chart will show in corresponding detail where the funding will be used, including the balance for necessary working capital. This exercise will illustrate that there is adequate money for the purchase price as well as projecting the demands for working capital after closing. Performing this exercise earlier rather than later will also help you determine whether the deal can be funded properly. It will save heartbreak if funds can't be assembled, and you will not waste money chasing a deal which can't be completed. Sometimes an acquisition just can't be finalized due to current economic circumstances or other economic cycles, and it's better to learn this before significant due-diligence monies and time are spent on a deal that won't happen.

Step 4

Calculate all transactions and deal costs.

Making errors in these costs is a common but disastrous mistake made even by seasoned business owners and operators. This happens because many potential costs are stealthy—until the closing date comes—and then, wham!

Examples of these expenses are:

- Closing bonuses paid to a litany of people, from bankers to employees;
- Broker's fees for the buyers and sometimes even the seller's side;
- Professional fees to accountants and lawyers;
- Interest expenses, banking due diligence and other closing fees the borrower always has to pay at closing. Depending on the deal structure or the purchase

agreement, these fees can easily reach six figures—even on smaller deals;

- Capital expenditures due to pre-existing restoration needs or projects started and not finished, or perhaps a roof in need of repair but which the seller didn't have the cash to pay for prior to closing;
- Past due payments directly related to manufacturing operations the seller had no plans to pay prior to closing;
- Possible inventory shortages;
- Past due accounts payable;
- Current taxes due on PP&E (plant, property, and equipment) or other specific taxes relating to a city, county, or state.

Step 5
Fully understand the three previous years of operating and financial history.

Three years is fair and insightful when trying to verify future projections. KPAC almost always buys businesses with a previous track record of negative Earnings Before Interest, Taxes, Depreciation, and Amortization (EBITDA). This normally is combined with at least one downward trend line for revenue, gross profits, and/or net income. Sometimes it is all three!

Step 6
List the historical or current problems the company is experiencing.

Sometimes a company faces an industry-wide problem, while other times the problem is within a geographical area or just specific to the company being acquired. For instance, if the company is a heating and air conditioning manufacturer in a slump due to a poor economy, discuss with the seller the revenue picture in light of the downward trend historically and in future expectations. Another problem within the air conditioning industry may be the weakened financial state of the dealer base which installs the equipment in homes, apartments, or office buildings. Are the accounts receivable slowing and stretching out from thirty to sixty days because the builder is also slow in paying?

By the time KPAC enters the acquisition process with its accelerated valuation approach and quick closing solution, there has been at least one of three serious issues existing:

1. Excess global capacity directly putting downward pressure on profit margins;
2. A competitor has much lower fixed or variable costs than the seller's;
3. A better process has been created or a superior product has been produced by a competitor.

Most important, though, is to establish in your mind the limiting factors to a valuation not born of emotion but instead from pure logic, supported and validated by historical financial statements. If the seller says, "Forget the historical financials—let me tell you about the wonderful rosy future," WATCH OUT! Believe me when I say don't buy with your heart. Buy only with your wallet supported by sound financial reports.

Step 7
Assess the liabilities you will inherit.

Because KPAC buys distressed manufacturers, we limit or completely eliminate certain liabilities. Examples are some accrued costs or reserves. Also ripe for isolation are the accounts payable, which are aged by the date of shipment or delivery. In accordance with GAAP or the company's general accounting policy, it's likely that any receivable over ninety days has already had a reserve taken against it. If this is not the case, ask why, and also ask if GAAP currently is being used in these financial statements. Hopefully, the financials will be audited, which eliminates a large amount of due diligence.

Reducing the purchase price by the negative values in a company's liabilities is a no-brainer the seller is almost forced to accept. However, it can be a challenge to find enough liabilities to get the price down as low as you want it—but every dollar counts. Each liability classification on the balance sheet is listed separately, just like on the asset side, so keep looking. KPAC always searches each classification for potential limiting capabilities which can directly affect the purchase price.

STEP 8
Evaluate each line of accounts receivable and inventory.

When KPAC values the assets of the potential acquisition, each line item separately identified is analyzed just like in Step #7, this time relating to accounts receivable. Each classification has its own level of difficulty when trying to convert it to cash. Like banks making a loan, KPAC discounts the entire accounts receivable by 10 or 15 percent. In addition, if one customer becomes overdue on an invoice, the entire group of invoices from that specific customer becomes worthless in the banker's way of valuation. KPAC doesn't take that strong or aggressive of a position in valuing accounts receivable, but we do require some concessions on receivables.

Although inventory is a complicated asset group to understand and value, it becomes more manageable if divided into three categories:

1. **Raw material** is a term applied to any material with no added value. It is unprocessed or unfinished goods, yet to be used by a manufacturer to make a finished product.
2. **WIP**—"Work In Process"—means something has affected or changed the raw material. This could be a

good thing or a bad thing in terms of its value. It depends on what happened and the type of raw material involved.

3. **Finished goods** also can be good or bad from a valuation standpoint. For instance, it is better to show popcorn machines that have been assembled and shipped to pre-paid customers than popcorn machines that have been completed but not yet shipped. And if the product is a component of the customer's product, the situation can be even more tenuous. If, for example, you are buying a company which makes custom car parts and the company is late shipping them to GM or Ford, you may find they are no longer needed because a customer this big gets tired of waiting and simply finds another vendor. The parts might have value sometime down the road but surely don't have the same inherent value as the finished popcorn machine.

Inventory can age on the shelf and still retain its value with respect to functionality. However, the problem might lie with obsolescence which, of course, could make it completely worthless. Or there may be an excessive amount of inventory which realistically will never be consumed or sold.

STEP 9
Consider the tax implications of the acquisition.

Of all topics discussed in this section, tax issues are the most important for which you should seek professional advice from a certified public accountant (CPA), especially if dealing with foreign-based operations. It is equally important if the seller is not a U.S. citizen. The burden of taxes owed to the U.S. government falls on the buyer's shoulders, so be sure to account for taxes due, and adjust the purchase price accordingly. How the acquisition is financed may also affect the purchase price.

For tax purposes, the IRS requires the buyer and seller to agree upon the purchase price tax allocation, which is the buyer's opening balance sheet (for tax) at the moment of closing, going forward. Known as purchase accounting, it is extremely important.

It also is crucial to understand what values are assigned to each asset classification so the proper depreciation schedules can be set up. The PP&E often includes many different lengths of depreciation, ranging from three to twenty years or more. The purchase price, which has a direct link to the opening balance sheet, will also limit certain tax relief and/or benefits tied together by the inside or outside tax manager or advisor.

The type of corporation selected immediately can have implications for a variety of reasons, especially if the forming entity owns other corporations. So be cautious in selecting the type of corporation for making an acquisition.

STEP 10
Analyze the company's debt.

Existing debt on the balance sheet is never a completely good thing, although the leveraging of equity with certain limited debt positions in an ongoing business does have its place. In recent years, off-balance-sheet financing has had horrendous negative repercussions on companies. The IRS ruled there is no such thing as an interest-free loan, so regardless of the extenuating circumstances, you must compute a reasonable interest rate and apply it to any debt on the balance sheet.

Debt normally requires a principal reduction and an interest charge that might change during the life of the loan. Both items may or may not be calculated on a fiscal year time period. Any and all debt, including lease payments (another form of debt handled differently on the balance sheet and with different tax ramifications), requires monthly, quarterly, or annual payments of some kind. Debt is either secured with specific collateral (including cross-collateralization) or unsecured without any collateral but with the company's written obligation to repay the debt plus interest within a certain period of time.

Finally, debt instruments can be formulated into sophisticated methods, including different balloon payments with variable interest rates tied to the U.S. Treasury and equity kickers, which substitute an applied interest rate with actual equity in the company. Some debt can be maintained off the balance sheet.

STEP 11
If you're not familiar with the industry, learn all you can about it before making an acquisition.

KPAC has sometimes gained advantages over other potential buyers because it buys only manufacturing companies. Since we specialize and know the true capabilities of most machinery and manufacturing processes so well, our management team has been able to spot irregular manpower allocations to jobs. We also have identified opportunities to make simple changes in the way a company does business resulting in increased profitability. The lesson here is to always take time to understand the elements of the specific industry of the potential acquisition, with an eye toward potential cost savings and increased earnings.

STEP 12
Use EBITDA to determine how much cash you will need to run the business.

During the last decade or so, EBITDA has become the standard formula for a quick calculation of free cash flow. At KPAC, though, we add another important calculation to our process. A more sophisticated formula reveals "net-free cash flow":

Net Free Cash Flow = Operation cash flow – Capital expenses to keep current level of operation – Dividends – Current portion of long-term debt – Depreciation

While EBITDA is a proven method with which a buyer can determine valuation, net-free cash flow allows the buyer to have a well-defined cash amount which the buyer will be truly free to use however he or she wants to spend it. If negative, it is the amount the buyer will need to supply to keep the business operating. (Be especially careful if this number is negative!)

Step 13
Use appropriate EBITDA multiples.

Using EBITDA to calculate a valuation for a potential acquisition is not just a simple decision of using three to five times the EBITDA. (However, this is a very common range used across many industries—with the exception of athletic clubs, contracting firms, and professional services like lawyers, doctors, and engineers.)

As a general rule, a proven growth-oriented company (either one in a new industry or perhaps a company making acquisitions) will demand a higher multiple of EBITDA than a company showing historically flat profitability. A higher multiple of the EBITDA can sometimes be justified if the potential acquisition demonstrates that the historical track record can be sustained going forward under new ownership. For example, if a company has $1 million in EBITDA, but has two acquisitions lined up (signed up would be better) which will increase the EBITDA by two more million, then a valuation of four, five, or more times the EBITDA would be appropriate. But don't be caught counting your chickens before they hatch!

Notwithstanding the above rules of thumb, there is no exact multiple times the EBITDA for forming a reliable valuation. For instance, a large customer might have been lost or gained in the historical year or the current fiscal year or even the next fiscal year, depending on when in the calendar year the offer is made. The value would be reduced for this problem; the question is: how much? Experience will help determine the answer.

An investment banker, CPA, or other trusted advisor may be able to provide valuable insight.

STEP 14
Use knowledge to your advantage.

Like most things in life, the art of negotiating is improved with practice. One way to gain a major negotiating advantage is to be knowledgeable about all aspects of the potential acquisition. Sometimes withholding information which can be bad or good for the company and then acknowledging or announcing it as a surprise can give one party an advantage. More times than not, however, I have seen that technique backfire. Making such a play suggests a company isn't acting in good faith (which, unfortunately, happens more than you would like to think with certified professionals involved). The person or company on the other end of the trickery feels he or she has been treated with disrespect or condescension. As a result, KPAC always tries to be upfront and avoid surprising the other party.

Observations about a particular company when compared to similar or identically operated companies can dramatically alter the valuation. For instance, suppose you have two dry cleaners on the same street. One is run-down, disorganized, and has poor customer service. The other is tidy, well run, and has friendly staff. Knowledge of these intangibles may persuade me to pay twice as much for the second dry cleaner than the one with shoddy operations and poor customer service.

STEP 15
Step back before moving forward.

Always let a comprehensive valuation analysis rest for a night (otherwise known as "let's sleep on it"). With my "do-it-now" nature, this has been a difficult discipline for me to learn. I have a history of pushing people to hurry up, which absolutely is not the best approach. My colleagues Bob Gielow and Kevin

Kennedy have taught me the value of waiting a day before submitting a valuation (thanks, guys), and many times, the next day we found errors ranging from a simple typo to huge mistakes, such as making calculations using the wrong currency or making a mathematical error which would have been nearly impossible to explain—or correct—without jeopardizing our reputations.

Appendix 2

The KPAC Solutions
Turnaround Model

W hile certain principles in the KPAC model may be applied to a variety of acquisition situations, the KPAC approach is designed specifically for companies meeting these two criteria:

1. The company is in the lower middle market—$5 million to $100 million in annual revenues;
2. It is a single, stand-alone company not relying on another company for its survival. However, it can have multiple plants and R&D or corporate offices located in another state—or even another country.

MERGERS AND ACQUISITIONS—GENERAL BACKGROUND

To understand the distinctives of KPAC's turnaround model, it is important to recognize the seller's circumstances when we first come on the scene. The characteristics of a seller from which KPAC usually buys a company or a division are:

- It is a public company or large private company highly motivated to sell the subsidiary or division;
- It has attempted, without success, to sell the business by itself or by using an investment banker as an intermediary.

Generally, the selling process through an investment banker ranges from four to ten months, and the number of parties seriously interested in acquiring the company will affect the timeline to closing. When more potential buyers are involved, the process usually takes longer.

In nearly every case, a potential buyer can be categorized into one of two groups: a strategic buyer or a financial buyer. The strategic buyer probably is already in the same business as the seller or is vertically integrated. The purpose of buying the company is to expand existing territorial boundaries or product offerings, sometimes both. A financial buyer is not necessarily in the same business and is more interested in a return on the investment. Both types will value the business based on their own perspective and goals.

Sometimes a business is put up for sale and goes through the normal selling process without finding a buyer. This outcome is called a "busted auction," and it usually is exasperating to all parties involved.

There are three circumstances which contribute significantly to negative earnings (normally expressed in EBITDA—Earnings Before Interest, Taxes, Depreciation, and Amortization):

1. There is an over-capacity of the manufactured product on a global scale;

2. The competitors have much cheaper variable and/or fixed costs;

3. The competitors develop "a better mouse trap" (i.e., process or design).

The KPAC Approach, KPAC's "Fast Lane"

KPAC's core strategy is to close a deal quickly. When the seller, a large company, owns a much smaller business facing any combination of the three problems noted above, it is often a sign to sell.

KPAC minimizes its own risk by buying assets and as little of everything else, including debt, as possible. The asset valuation is largely completed by discounting assets similar to the way a bank would when establishing a lending base. KPAC is able to have an accelerated closing timeline because of 1) our conservative approach to estimating the value of the assets through a liquidation analysis; 2) the seller's indemnification; and 3) the reduced amount of due diligence required thanks to our knowledge of the manufacturing industry.

Dealing only with audited financial statements by a large accounting firm adds an additional assurance that the assets are valued correctly on the most current balance sheet (assuming the last audit is current within the most recent fiscal year).

An additional security blanket is the federal law, Sarbanes Oxley, which holds the executive officers of a public company accountable for any misrepresentations found in the audited financial statements filed with the Securities and Exchange Commission (SEC). The company's quarterly and annually audited financial statements—required by law to be filed with the SEC and signed by the top financial officer and top board members—provide a great deal of insight into the operations and holdings of the entity as well, and they offer the added security of top management's signatures.

KPAC is committed to producing a written, binding quote within seventy-two hours of receiving appropriate information about a company's finances and operations. A public company has a reputation to maintain, and the sellers we work with want to make sure the acquiring company doesn't do anything to embarrass them. As a result, it is vital the seller understand KPAC can move quickly because of our expertise, not because we are reckless and taking unwarranted risk in the closing process.

Most sellers have a comfort level with KPAC not only because of our proven track record, but also because they recognize we conservatively value the assets and substantially reduce our risk with liabilities. Our challenge is getting a seller to consider allowing KPAC the privilege of making an offer.

KPAC usually does not acquire through the investment banker auction process (I lost too much money the few times I tried), although once we went through the process to buy a company out of bankruptcy. But that time, the deck was stacked in our favor.

KPAC doesn't spend time or money validating a public company's financial statements, because essentially we would be replicating the same auditing function already done when the financials were prepared. We do, however, hold the seller accountable if there are discrepancies between what the seller previously reported and our master purchase agreement, compared to what we actually get at closing.

As part of our due diligence, KPAC visits the potential acquisition's facilities, and we try to meet with management at least once to determine their competency. But our visits are quick. We don't spend time standing in one place too long, and we don't take notes. We try to look like "regular people" touring the place.

In every purchase so far, we have had access to the management team running the company. On rare occasions, an upper-level manager or an employee important to the seller in one of its other, unrelated businesses will choose not to become part of our new team. Otherwise, all employees become part of the new ownership structure. This is helpful to the seller, because it eliminates employees from asking for a transfer to other divisions or to companies within the seller's other businesses.

KPAC is loyal to the finder of the completed acquisition. If the finder is an investment banker, we attempt to use it first when we go back into the market to sell. KPAC pays handsome finder's fees, sometimes reaching seven figures if the acquisition is large enough to warrant it. The balance sheet and the revenue stream have a major influence on what the finder's fee becomes.

Over the years, KPAC's track record has demonstrated to public sellers that we know what we are doing and that we will do what we say. One reason is that not having a bankruptcy in our past means one less potential embarrassment for the seller after closing the deal. Second, KPAC has never completely closed down or bankrupted any of our acquisitions, which gains us favor even if we don't have the highest offer on the table.

We have discovered that the more transparency we have with the seller, the more insight the seller has into our day-to-day decisions, and the faster we move, the more transparency becomes a crucial factor because it promotes trust and goodwill. Even after closing, we often offer transparency through the outside auditor's post-closing work. We always try to employ the same outside auditors to assure a seamless pre- to post-closing transition. This also eliminates some of the evaluation process sellers might think they have to do.

Part of our valuation strategy might include a "still in business" payment as an incentive to accept our offer. This one-time back-end or delayed payment is typically twenty-four months after closing, assuming the business is still operating normally. If we can turn the business around in a short period of time, we can generate a substantial portion of that back-end payment through revenues.

ALL, NOT NOTHING

"All inclusive" is often a critical component of our offer. These two magical words can be the key to our winning the acquisition. Within the M&A industry, "cherry-picking" is frowned upon, but many buyers try it anyway. Cherry-picking is a temptation because often a company—especially a larger company with multiple plant locations—will contain assets which are undesirable because of their location, age, condition, or profitability. Buyers offer to purchase only specified assets or operations. Since this means some components of the company stay with the seller, it leaves the seller with still more assets to dispose of after the initial sale.

The last thing a seller wants to do is sell a business in pieces unless there are clear advantages to doing so. Most times, the seller simply wants a distressed, busted-auction business or division to disappear. The KPAC silver bullet of buying the entire company has enabled us to pull past competitors without having the highest valuation or quickest payment schedule, simply because our acquisition price includes everything. The cleaner and easier we make it for the seller, the more likely KPAC's offer will be chosen.

THE ADVANTAGES OF STICKING WITH WHAT YOU KNOW

As I mentioned earlier, KPAC only purchases manufacturing companies since we are experts in this field. Each deal stands on its own, with a new corporation formed each time to hold the acquisition prior to closing. Buying manufacturers gives us confidence in rules of thumb which only apply to the manufacturing industry.

For instance, we can see a picture or be given a description of a piece of equipment. Even though the book might say the equipment can produce x number of pieces per hour, or is the best that money can buy, KPAC might know better. In fact, we may have actually owned that piece of equipment in a previous acquisition. By knowing the manufacturing sector inside and out, we can breeze through volumes of due diligence because we have already experienced much of it first hand. It is far easier to remember something days or weeks later if you already know the facts about it from another transaction. So whatever business you know best, stick to acquisitions within your industry.

Our strategy is to establish our high level of manufacturing expertise with the seller as quickly as possible. By doing this, the seller may suspect that KPAC knows more about the equipment and processes used, including distribution choices and the over-all business, than the current owners. This gives us an advantage when we discount the equipment or make comments about better and/or quicker manufacturing methods. However, we are careful not to come across as arrogant or having a know-it-all attitude. We always strive to be humble, polite, patient, and kind to the seller's representatives—and everyone else.

Our commitment to run our business honorably doesn't impede our ability to be aggressive, candid, and forthright with our business model. Our temperament can change quickly, especially after closing when tough decisions must be made in order to turn the ailing business around.

One Hundred Days to Profitability

Employee morale of an acquired company can be a roller coaster before we gain control at closing. Therefore, it is important to convey a steady and consistent management profile at all times because of KPAC's commitment to our "One Hundred Days to Profitability" strategy. The phrase and timeline of one hundred days is intended to convey a mandate for change. This change can be as major as closing an entire plant or eliminating half of the product offering. The main focus during this period is to be left with a company that has a clean business model and the resources necessary to be both competitive and profitable.

The acquisition's vendors and suppliers can affect our One Hundred Days to Profitability positively or negatively. However, the employee base, customer base, vendor, or material-suppliers base (including sub-assemblies, if applicable), and freightliners are all asked to participate in our strategy of finding some amount of cost savings.

After signing the letter of intent, KPAC immediately asks for more detailed financial information so we can build our own financial model. We always reassure the seller that KPAC is not asking for financial back-up to renegotiate the purchase price. KPAC uses a sophisticated outline to generate its own financial modeling. The more detail, the better we like it. The first one hundred days are critical in our minds to establishing the new company with a business plan which will make it profitable as soon as possible.

KPAC's pre-acquisition efforts are aimed at being ready, as much as possible, to assume operational control on day one of the acquisition. The more prepared we are prior to the closing, the better we like it.

CHECKLIST OF WHAT YOU NEED TO KNOW

The following is based on the assumption that no traditional debt is assumed from the seller, including equipment leases. There are eleven primary areas of a company for which KPAC requests information prior to the actual closing date:

1. Audited financial statements for the last three years, including three years of forecasted fiscal years with annualized capital expenditures;
2. Raw material purchases, including sub-assemblies from a vendor base or sub-assembler(s) and associated freight rates;
3. Detailed profit margin(s) of product offerings by customer and geographical regions;

4. Existing inventory level(s), again with comprehensive detail including aging by product or part number and WIP (Work In Process);

5. Finished goods, with the same level of detail as inventory, including connected freight cost by customer and freight line/carrier(s);

6. Accounts receivable, with their aging by customer;

7. Customer base with as much detail as possible, including their physical location, mailing address if different than physical location, products purchased, annual volume, and profit margins;

8. Complete equipment list of what is in the plant, the age of each piece, and the ownership or lease status and terms;

9. The plant and building age and square footage, the ownership or lease status and terms, and acreage, including current or near-term capacity issues;

10. Technologies, patents with detailed status of each, what country it is registered in, and the date of expected expiration;

11. Organizational chart showing every existing employee with compensation and the latest increase in compensation.

SPECIAL CONSIDERATIONS FOR INTERNATIONAL ACQUISITIONS

When dealing with an acquisition that has international operations—especially when it is headquartered abroad—KPAC must complete due diligence for terminating employees and their respective unions. Likewise, environmental regulations vary around the world and merit careful analysis prior to making an acquisition.

KPAC has owned plants in Europe, North America, Latin America, and China. Very few other private equity firms can claim to do what KPAC can do under the $150 million valuation range. Our main competitors have raised multiple billions in private equity funds with the requirement that they acquire much larger companies, in the half-billion dollar range.

STREAMLINING THE PURCHASE

KPAC's initial approach was borne out of limited travel funds as well as the cost of chasing a potential acquisition through the traditional investment banker process. Too often for me, my efforts were thwarted by financially stronger buyers. Sometimes my competition was a public company using its own publicly traded stock to help make the acquisition. This was a tax advantage because the seller could trade its stock for the buyer's public stock without any taxable income. KPAC's offer was always taxable because we are a private company, and trading for our stock didn't provide sellers with the liquidity they desired.

Today, KPAC's strategy is to get an offer in front of the seller without it costing us an arm and a leg. We refuse to enter into the process an investment banker creates, which is designed to get the seller the maximum amount at closing. KPAC will make an offer at the end—or afterwards if the process was not successful. Usually, the standard process works well for the investment bankers, but when it doesn't, KPAC stands ready to come to the table with a binding offer. By the time we arrive, sellers always welcome having an offer, but our purchase price usually gives them heartburn.

When everyone else has walked away from the deal, KPAC comes to the table focused on speed and responsiveness. Our quickness to respond becomes addictive to sellers; the more they get a taste of our speed, the better our chances become of getting a deal completed. We're often amazed (and a bit gratified) to see how shocked our competitors who went through the auction process are when they see at how low a price we buy the business.

Many times, the acquisition was in such a state of disrepair we were paid to take the company, because its problems were too big to solve within the necessary timeframe. Sometimes, the business was losing so much money the seller had to fund the losses long enough to allow us to stop the red ink and turn the company around.

On many occasions, sellers chose KPAC because we were willing to take all the employees in countries known for high redundancy (severance) costs. We would simply ask the seller to fund the redundancy costs on the balance sheet prior to closing. This allowed us to handle it after closing, long after the seller was out of the picture and would not be embarrassed by the termination of employees.

More times than not, KPAC re-hires terminated employees prior to later selling the business to a strategic or financial buyer. Sometimes, we have more employees when we sell a company than when we first purchased it.

KPAC always produces an offer with other vital information to help the seller understand our proposal. We include the timeframe divided into three or four easy steps so the buyer can quickly understand our strategy, and we provide candid assessments (some might even think us rude) of the problems as we see them. We list by topic what due diligence is needed and the timeframe of information we are seeking.

KPAC always makes our indemnifications as short as possible. This is done to get the seller's attention that we really are serious about the acquisition, and we will not be bogged down in tons of due-diligence requests and then ask for additional time for outside auditors. In fact, KPAC has never used outside auditors in any of our deals.

I recommend our system because it works. To date, we still have never closed a business down completely or filed for bankruptcy with one. And our ability to claim that keeps on building credibility with potential sellers.

For more information about KPAC's model, visit www.kpacsolutions.com.

Appendix 3

Make a You Turn

I f you're going in the wrong direction spiritually and realize you need to make a "you turn," it's important to know what it takes to get re-started in the right direction. Dr. C. Gordon Olson, in his book *Getting the Gospel Right*, offers this helpful analogy to explain the critical difference between repentance and conversion:

When one is driving down the interstate, repentance is the realization that one is going in the wrong direction. Conversion is when one finds an exit and makes a u-turn.

"A Step of FAITH*" below explains how you can receive Jesus Christ as your personal savior. I am grateful to LifeWay Christian Resources for granting permission to reprint it here.

---

* "A Step of Faith" © 2007 LifeWay Christian Resources. Used by permission.

A STEP OF FAITH

Jesus loves you and wants to have a personal relationship with you. In your personal opinion, what do you understand it takes for a person to get to heaven and have eternal life?

Here is how the Bible answers this question. It is answered in one word, and the word is FAITH.

F IS FOR FORGIVENESS

- Everyone has sinned and needs God's forgiveness. Romans 3:23: "All have sinned and fall short of the glory of God."
- God's forgiveness is in Jesus only. Ephesians 1:7: "In Him we have redemption through His blood, the forgiveness of our trespasses, according to the riches of His grace."

A IS FOR AVAILABLE

- God's forgiveness is available for all. John 3:16: "God loved the world in this way: He gave His One and Only Son, so that everyone who believes in Him will not perish but have eternal life."
- God's forgiveness is available but not automatic. Matthew 7:21: "Not everyone who says to Me, 'Lord, Lord!' will enter the kingdom of heaven."

I IS FOR IMPOSSIBLE

- According to the Bible, it is impossible to get to heaven on our own. Ephesians 2:8-9: "By grace you are saved through faith, and this is not from yourselves; it is God's gift—not from works, so that no one can boast."

So how can a sinful person have eternal life and enter heaven?

T Is for TURN

- If you were going down the road and someone asked you to turn, what would he or she be asking you to do? Change direction. Turn means repent. Turn away from sin and self. Luke 13:3: "Unless you repent, you will all perish as well!"
- Turn to Jesus alone as your Savior and Lord. John 14:6: "I am the way, the truth, and the life. No one comes to the Father except through Me."
- Here is the greatest news of all. Romans 10:9-10: "If you confess with your mouth, 'Jesus is Lord,' and believe in your heart that God raised Him from the dead, you will be saved. With the heart one believes, resulting in righteousness, and with the mouth one confesses, resulting in salvation."

What happens if a person is willing to repent of their sins and confess Christ?

H Is for HEAVEN

- Heaven is a place where we will live with God forever. John 14:3: "If I go away and prepare a place for you, I will come back and receive you to Myself, so that where I am you may be also."
- Eternal life begins now with Jesus. John 10:10: "I have come that they may have life and have it in abundance."

H can also stand for HOW.

- How can a person have God's forgiveness, eternal life, and heaven? By trusting Jesus as your Savior and Lord. You can do this right now by praying and asking Jesus to forgive you of your sins and inviting Jesus into your heart.

- Accepting Christ is just the beginning of a wonderful adventure with God! Get to know Him better in a number of ways:
- Follow Christ's example in baptism.
- Join a church where you can worship God and grow in your faith.
- In your church, get involved in Sunday School and Bible study.
- Begin a daily personal worship experience with God where you study the Bible and pray.

LaVergne, TN USA
07 October 2010
199850LV00001B/1/P